Interprocess Communication with macOS

Apple IPC Methods

Hem Dutt

Apress®

Interprocess Communication with macOS: Apple IPC Methods

Hem Dutt
North Delhi, Delhi, India

ISBN-13 (pbk): 978-1-4842-7044-8   ISBN-13 (electronic): 978-1-4842-7045-5
https://doi.org/10.1007/978-1-4842-7045-5

Managing Director, Apress Media LLC: Welmoed Spahr
Acquisitions Editor: Aaron Black
Development Editor: James Markham
Coordinating Editor: Jessica Vakili

Distributed to the book trade worldwide by Springer Science+Business Media New York,
1 NY Plaza, New York, NY 10014. Phone 1-800-SPRINGER, fax (201) 348-4505, e-mail orders-ny@springer-sbm.com, or visit www.springeronline.com. Apress Media, LLC is a California LLC and the sole member (owner) is Springer Science + Business Media Finance Inc (SSBM Finance Inc). SSBM Finance Inc is a **Delaware** corporation.

For information on translations, please e-mail booktranslations@springernature.com; for reprint, paperback, or audio rights, please e-mail bookpermissions@springernature.com.

Apress titles may be purchased in bulk for academic, corporate, or promotional use. eBook versions and licenses are also available for most titles. For more information, reference our Print and eBook Bulk Sales web page at http://www.apress.com/bulk-sales.

Any source code or other supplementary material referenced by the author in this book is available to readers on GitHub via the book's product page, located at www.apress.com/978-1-4842-7044-8. For more detailed information, please visit http://www.apress.com/source-code.

Printed on acid-free paper

This book is dedicated to all the students and fellow software engineers who want to explore more about macOS and interprocess communication.

I would also like to dedicate this book to my parents who nurtured and disciplined my life.

Last but not the least, I would like to dedicate this book to my beloved wife Payal who gave a new meaning to my life, kept me motivated for new ventures, and without whom this was not possible.

Table of Contents

About the Author

 **Hem Dutt** started his software engineering career in 2010 as an OS X application developer and, thereafter, designed and developed numerous native macOS and iOS applications for various clients across the globe while working in multiple MNCs. With a continuous experience of more than a decade on OS X, Hem Dutt worked in multiple domains, which include healthcare, insurance, VPN clients, publishing, and IOT. During his work in all these domains, he got the chance to work extensively on IPC and privilege elevation problems. His passion for designing and developing secure, reliable, and modular software is evident from his blogs, client awards/recommendations, and open source projects.

He created and maintains `https://techknowmore.wordpress.com` and `https://github.com/HemDutt`.

About the Technical Reviewer

Felipe Laso is a Senior Systems Engineer working at Lextech Global Services. He's also an aspiring game designer/programmer. You can follow him on Twitter at @iFeliLM or on his blog.

Acknowledgments

I have to start by thanking my awesome wife, Payal, for keeping me motivated throughout my journey as a writer. She is always by my side and pushes me to fulfill my dreams however impossible they seem to others. Thank you so much dear for being my pillar of strength. You are a superwoman.

I must offer special thanks to my parents who nurtured my childhood and despite their limited means provided me the best they could possibly do and shaped my character.

I would also like to thank Aaron Black and Apress for giving me this opportunity, and special mention to Jessica Vakili for supporting and guiding me throughout the development of this book.

A big thanks to technical and editorial reviewers for helping me in shaping the chapters and content of this book.

I would also like to thank my colleagues and friends, who always believed in me and encouraged me. Special mention to Team Firefighters. It was a pleasure working with you guys and a learning experience.

A special thanks to a very special person, Dr. Thomas Griffin, for being a mentor, friend, and a guru to me. You have helped me grow, and I must acknowledge your contribution in what I am today.

Finally, I would like to acknowledge my two beautiful children, Anika and Adwit. Thanks Anika for being such a powerhouse and for bringing so much energy into the house and Adwit for being such a sweetheart and adorable baby and filling the atmosphere with unconditional love. I love both of you so much.

CHAPTER 1

Introduction to IPC on macOS

In the computing world, processes execute to accomplish specified computation. A process which is acting independently does not get affected by the execution of other processes. Though it seems that the processes that are running independently will execute very efficiently and are less error prone, in reality, there could be many situations when cooperative processes can be utilized for increasing modularity, computational speed, and convenience but at the cost of increased complexity.

An effective way to use a computer system is to spread the given computation over several processes. To achieve more speed and modularity, processes need to work and communicate in parallel and distributed processing environments. These processes then form a set of communicating processes which cooperate in computing to reach a solution. In a highly distributed, multiprocessor system, these processes may even reside on different machines. In such a case, the communication is supported over a network.

With cooperation, complexity increases and the need for **interprocess communication (IPC)** arises.

© Hem Dutt 2021
H. Dutt, *Interprocess Communication with macOS*,
https://doi.org/10.1007/978-1-4842-7045-5_1

Interprocess Communication

Interprocess communication (IPC) is the set of techniques provided by the operating system to allow processes to communicate with each other.

This communication could be about a process notifying another process about some event or the transferring of data from one process to another.

Alternatively, it can be defined as the set of techniques used for exchanging data or messages among multiple threads in one or more processes. Processes may be running on one or more computers and may or may not be connected by a network.

Typically, applications and processes involved in IPC are categorized as the clients and servers, where the client requests data and the server responds to client requests.

It is possible that among the participating applications and processes in IPC, some always act like the server, while others always act like the client. It is also possible that participating applications or processes can change their role and selectively become the client and the server during various computation flows.

Many applications and processes are both clients and servers, as commonly seen in distributed computing.

IPC is integral to the design of microkernels and nanokernels, which segregate the kernel services into the user address space and the kernel address space and bus limit the number of functionalities provided by the kernel.

A microkernel provides only minimal services of process and memory management. The communication between the client program and services running in the user address space is established through IPC techniques.

The advantage is that the operating system remains unaffected as user services and kernel services are isolated, and so if any user service fails, it does not affect the kernel service. Thus, a microkernel is easily extendable, and if any new services are to be added, they can be added into the user address space and so require no modification in kernel space. It makes it portable, secure, and reliable.

An IPC mechanism can be categorized as synchronous or asynchronous. Synchronization in IPC is either provided by the interprocess control mechanism or handled by the communicating processes. The following are the methods that can be used to have synchronous behavior with an asynchronous IPC mechanism and are known as synchronization primitives:

- **Semaphore**: A semaphore is an integer variable that controls the access to a common resource by multiple processes. Semaphores are used to solve the critical section problem by using two atomic operations, wait and signal. Semaphores can be further categorized into binary semaphores and counting semaphores.

- **Mutual exclusion**: Mutual exclusion or mutex is a concurrency control mechanism which prevents race conditions. It enforces that a process does not enter its critical section while another parallel process is currently executing its critical section.

- **Barrier**: A barrier for a group of threads or processes does not allow individual processes to proceed until all the processes reach it. Many directive-based parallel languages and collective routines impose barriers.

- **Spinlock**: A spinlock is a type of lock which makes a thread trying to acquire it to wait in a loop ("spin") while repeatedly checking if the lock is available. Since the thread remains active but does not perform a useful task during this time, this lock mechanism falls into the busy waiting category.

IPC on macOS

Building a highly modular software is always tricky, and complexity only increases when the program is interacting with another program. If the interprocess communication (IPC) is poorly conceived and carried out, it can lead to severe security risks not just for the participating programs but for the overall system. A poorly conceived IPC can expose the entire system for the hackers and other over-the-network attacks.

With increasing complexity of software applications and their dependencies on reusable frameworks/libraries, usually, at some point in its life cycle, a process or an application needs to communicate in some way with another process or application.

On macOS, there are multiple scenarios where implementing IPC between two or more processes/applications is necessary. These scenarios can be broadly categorized into five categories:

1. **Information sharing**: Applications and processes share data among themselves to synchronize their actions and flows.

2. **Computational speedup**: This includes sending data off-site for processing. High-volume computations are delegated to off-site servers, and results were shown through the on-site application.

3. **Modularity**: Google Chrome, for example, implements this by separating each tab into a separate process. This helps avoid crashes and augment security.

4. **Convenience**: More often than not, multiple developers work on an application simultaneously and design and develop different processes in parallel. It is thus easier to have multiple teams

build separate processes keeping IPC in mind and then essentially "plug in" the processes in one or more applications as needed.

5. **Privilege separation**: By default, on macOS, applications run as the currently logged in user. Different users have different rights when it comes to accessing files, changing system-wide settings, and so on, depending on whether they are admin users or ordinary users.

   For increasing security and protection from attacks like buffer overflow, access control problems, weaknesses in authentication, authorization, or cryptographic practices, and so on, even admin users are restricted from running certain tasks.

   Some tasks like opening privileged ports, creating shared secure keychain items for VPN connections, and so on require additional privileges above and beyond what even an admin user can do by default.

   An application or other processes with such additional rights are said to be running with elevated privileges. Running code with root or administrative privileges can intensify the dangers posed by security vulnerabilities. And so to elevate privileges safely, it is mandatory for the application to perform tasks through a secure helper process.

   The communication between the application and the secure helper process is carried out by IPC techniques.

IPC Techniques on macOS

In many ways, the story of Apple has been about fusing together technologies throughout its history to create something better than before.

For example, OS X came up as a hybrid of macOS and NeXTSTEP. Objective-C was Smalltalk's OOP paradigm and C. iCloud came as the by-product of MobileMe and actual clouds.

While many of these fusions were happy accidents for many aspects of Apple's technology stack, interprocess communication is a counterexample.

At every intersection, IPC solutions just piled up. As a result, overlapping, mutually incompatible IPC technologies are scattered across various abstraction layers ranging from low-level kernel abstractions to high-level, object-oriented APIs having their own particular performance and security characteristics.

Each of the IPC techniques available on macOS often has its own specific purposes, limitations, and intended scenarios. Some are more suitable than others for a certain level of the system. For example, a kernel extension would not make use of Apple Events.

In this chapter, we will have a brief overview of various techniques available on Mac to accomplish IPC. In the subsequent chapters, we will discuss each technique in detail with their use cases and will also look into the implementation of these techniques.

Shared File

Shared files are the most basic solution for implementing IPC where multiple processes will share a common file. It could be a simple txt file or a SQLite database. The obvious problems in this method are that

1. Clients need to continuously poll to see if the server has written something in the file.

2. Write problems if multiple processes are trying to write to the shared file at the same time.

6

We will not discuss this approach in isolation, but we can see this approach working in the case of app groups. App groups allow multiple apps produced by a single development team to access shared containers. One of the major example of this technique in action is data sharing between an iOS app and it's extensions.

Shared Memory

Shared memory is another implementation for IPC where a memory section is shared between different processes. In other words, process A writes to this memory, and process B can read from this memory, or vice versa. This is fast and data doesn't have to be copied around. The downside is that it's really difficult to coordinate changes to the shared memory area.

Mach Ports

Mach ports are the fundamental services, and primitives of the OS X kernel are based on Mach 3.0. Mach 3.0 was originally conceived as a simple, extensible, communications microkernel.

It is capable of running as a stand-alone kernel, with other traditional operating system services such as I/O, file systems, and networking stacks running as user-mode servers.

However, in OS X, Mach is linked with other kernel components into a single kernel address space. This is primarily for performance as it is much faster to make a direct call between linked components than it is to send messages or do remote procedure calls (RPC) between separate tasks.

This modular structure results in a more robust and extensible system than a monolithic kernel would allow, without the performance penalty of a pure microkernel.

The only disadvantage of Mach ports is complexity of implementation and less documentation.

Sockets

While most TCP/IP connections are established over a network between two different machines, it is also possible to connect two processes running on the same machine without ever touching a network using TCP/IP.

Using TCP/IP sockets for IPC is not very different from using them for network communications. In fact, they can be used in exactly the same way. But if the intent is only for local IPC, create a socket in the AF_UNIX family to get a socket that's only for local communication and uses more flexible addressing than TCP/IP allows.

Apple Events

Apple Events are the only IPC mechanism which is universally supported by GUI applications on macOS for remote control. Operations like telling an application to open a file or to quit can be done using these.

AppleScript is a scripting language built on top of Apple Events which can be used using Scripting Bridge in a Mac application.

Distributed Notifications

A notification center manages the sending and receiving of notifications. It notifies all observers of notifications meeting the specific criteria. The notification information is encapsulated in NSNotification objects.

Client objects register themselves with the notification center as observers of specific notifications posted by other objects. When an event occurs, an object posts an appropriate notification to the notification center.

Posting a distributed notification is an expensive operation. The notification gets sent to a system-wide server that then distributes it to all the processes that have objects registered for distributed notifications.

The latency between posting the notification and the notification's arrival in another process is unbounded. In fact, if too many notifications are being posted and the server's queue fills up, notifications can be dropped.

Pasteboard

Every time a copy-paste happens between applications, that's IPC happening using a pasteboard. Inter-application drag and drop also uses the pasteboard. It is possible to create custom pasteboards which only desired applications can access for passing data back and forth between applications.

Like distributed notifications, pasteboards work by talking to a central pasteboard server using Mach ports.

XPC

This is the latest technique provided by macOS. Before XPC, a common way to use IPC and provide services between processes was through Sockets, Mach messages, or distributed objects. Apple now encourages developers to use XPC in applications and frameworks that provide services. Also, Apple has updated many of its frameworks, daemons, and applications to use XPC.

XPC provides us with a new level of abstraction for IPC. But aside from providing an easier to use IPC mechanism, XPC also gives us some additional benefits that we will discuss in a later chapter.

Apart from the preceding techniques, in the last two chapters, we will discuss about the IPC between native and web applications and privileged Helper tools, respectively.

Summary

In the next chapters, we will discuss the briefly discussed IPC techniques in detail and will have some fun implementing these techniques in code. Stay tuned!

CHAPTER 2

IPC Through Shared Memory

As discussed briefly in Chapter 1, shared memory is an implementation for IPC where a memory section is shared between different processes. In other words, process A writes to the shared memory segment, and process B can read from this memory segment, or vice versa. In this chapter, we will go through concepts of shared memory and its implementation for IPC in detail.

Introduction to Shared Memory

In an IPC scenario, each participating process has its own address space. Just in case any process wants to pass some information or data from its address space to other processes, then it must implement IPC techniques to line up communication between related or unrelated processes (see Figure 2-1).

© Hem Dutt 2021
H. Dutt, *Interprocess Communication with macOS*,
https://doi.org/10.1007/978-1-4842-7045-5_2

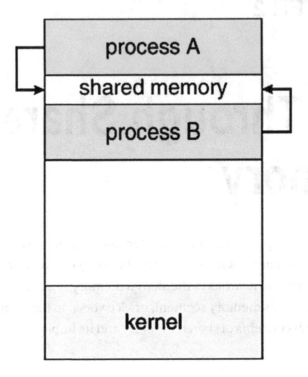

Figure 2-1. *Sample IPC scenario*

Usually, an interrelated process communication is performed using pipes or named pipes. The issue with pipes is that for two processes to exchange information, the data needs to traverse through the kernel.

1. First, the server process reads data from the input source.

2. Then the server process writes this data employing a pipe implementation.

3. Then the client process reads this data from the IPC channel. This again required the information to be copied from the kernel's IPC buffer to the client process buffer.

4. Finally, the data is copied from the client process buffer.

A total of four copies of data are required, that is, two reads and two writes. On the contrary, in such scenarios, shared memory provides a faster approach by letting processes share a memory segment. With shared memory, the information is merely copied twice—from the input source into shared memory and from shared memory to the output.

This provides a quick approach to IPC as data doesn't copy around. The downside is that it's really difficult to coordinate changes to the shared memory area. The complexity increases exponentially with each participating process.

Understanding System Calls

While performing IPC through shared memory, we will be using a few system calls. Let's have a brief overview of the concerned system calls and their usage strategies.

shmget

This system call creates a "System V" memory segment. A shared memory segment is created if either the key is equal to IPC_PRIVATE or the key does not have a shared memory segment identifier and the IPC_CREAT bit is set in shmflg (Listing 2-1).

On successful completion, a positive shared memory segment identifier is returned. Else, –1 is returned and the global variable errno is set to indicate the error (Table 2-2). Function arguments are explained in detail in Table 2-1.

Listing 2-1. shmget

```
#include <sys/shm.h>
int shmget(key_t key, size_t size, int shmflg);
```

Table 2-1. *Function arguments*

Function Arguments	Description
key	The first argument "key" is an identifier for the shared memory segment. The key could be an arbitrary value, or it can be derived from the library function ftok().
	The key can be IPC_PRIVATE as well, which means that running processes needs to have parent child relationship.
	If the client process wants to use shared memory with this key, then it must be a child process of the server process which implies that the client process needs to be created after the parent has obtained a shared memory.
size	The second argument "size" is the size of the shared memory segment rounded to the multiple of PAGE_SIZE.
shmflg	The third argument "shmflg" is for the required shared memory flags such as IPC_CREAT or IPC_EXCL. The last nine bits of "shmflg" specify the permissions granted to the owner or group.

Table 2-2 provides the description of error codes in case of failure.

Table 2-2. *Errors*

Error Code	Description
EACCES	A shared memory segment is already associated with a key, and the caller has no permission to access it.
EEXIST	Both IPC_CREAT and IPC_EXCL are set in shmflg, and a shared memory segment is already associated with a key.

(continued)

Table 2-2. (*continued*)

Error Code	Description
EINVAL	No shared memory segment is to be created, and a shared memory segment exists for a key, but the size of the segment associated with it is less than the size, which is nonzero.
ENOENT	IPC_CREAT was not set in shmflg, and no shared memory segment associated with a key was found.
ENOMEM	There is not enough memory left to create a shared memory segment of the requested size.
ENOSPC	A new shared memory identifier could not be created because the system limit for the number of shared memory identifiers has been reached.

shmat

This system call attaches a shared memory segment to the address space of the calling process. It returns the address at which the shared memory segment has been mapped into the calling process's address space when successful (see Listing 2-2). Function arguments are described in Table 2-3. In case of failure, the global variable errno is set to indicate the error (Table 2-4).

Listing 2-2. shmat

```
#include <sys/shm.h>
void *shmat(int shmid, const void *shmaddr, int shmflg);
```

Table 2-3. *Function arguments*

Function Arguments	Description
shmid	The first argument "shmid" is an identifier for the shared memory segment.
shmaddr	The second argument "shmaddr" is for specifying the attaching address. If shmaddr is NULL, this means the system will by default choose the suitable address to attach the segment. If shmaddr is not NULL and SHM_RND is specified in shmflg, the attach is equal to the address of the nearest multiple of SHMLBA (lower boundary address). Otherwise, shmaddr must be a page-aligned address at which the shared memory attachment starts.
shmflg	The third argument "shmflg" specifies the required shared memory flags such as SHM_RND, SHM_EXEC, SHM_RDONLY, etc. A shared memory segment can be mapped read-only by specifying the SHM_RDONLY flag in shmflg.

Table 2-4. *Errors*

Error Code	Description
EACCES	The calling process has no permission to access this shared memory segment.
EINVAL	shmid is not a valid shared memory identifier. shmaddr specifies an illegal address.
EMFILE	The number of shared memory segments has reached the system-wide limit.
ENOMEM	There is not enough available data space for the calling process to map the shared memory segment.

shmdt

shmdt detaches the shared memory segment from the address space of the calling process.

It returns 0 on successful completion (Listing 2-3). Otherwise, a value of –1 is returned, and the global variable errno is set to indicate the error (Table 2-6). The function argument is described in Table 2-5.

Table 2-5. *Function argument*

Function Argument	Description
shmaddr	shmaddr is the address of the shared memory segment to be detached and must be the address returned by the shmat() system call.

Listing 2-3. shmdt

```
#include <sys/shm.h>
int shmdt(const void *shmaddr);
```

Table 2-6. *Error*

Error Code	Description
EINVAL	shmaddr is not the start address of a mapped shared memory segment.

shmctl

shmctl performs control operations on the shared memory area specified by shmid (Listing 2-4). Each shared memory segment has a data structure associated with it, parts of which may be altered by shmctl() and parts of which determine the actions of shmctl(). Function arguments are described in Table 2-8.

17

Listing 2-4. shmctl

```
#include <sys/shm.h>
int shmctl(int shmid, int cmd, struct shmid_ds *buf);
```

struct shmid_ds is defined in Listing 2-5.

Listing 2-5. shmid_ds

```
struct shmid_ds {
    /* operation permissions */
        struct ipc_perm  shm_perm;
    /* size of segment in bytes */
        int              shm_segsz;
    /* pid of last shm op */
        pid_t            shm_lpid;
    /* pid of creator */
        pid_t            shm_cpid;
    /* # of current attaches */
        short            shm_nattch;
    /* last shmat() time*/
        time_t           shm_atime;
    /* last shmdt() time */
        time_t           shm_dtime;
    /* last change by shmctl() */

        time_t           shm_ctime;
    /* sysv stupidity */
        void             *shm_internal;
    };
```

The ipc_perm structure used inside the shmid_ds structure is defined
in <sys/ipc.h> as in Listing 2-6.

Listing 2-6. ipc_perm

```
struct ipc_perm {
    /* Owner's user ID */
    uid_t           uid;
    /* Owner's group ID */
    gid_t           gid;
    /* Creator's user ID */
    uid_t           cuid;
    /* Creator's group ID */
    gid_t           cgid;
    /* r/w permission*/
    mode_t          mode;
    /* Reserved for internal use */
    unsigned short  _seq;
    /* Reserved for internal use */
    key_t           _key;
  };
```

The operation to be performed by shmctl() is specified in cmd, that is, the second parameter, and the value is one of the values listed in Table 2-7.

Table 2-7. *Types of cmd*

cmd Type	Description
IPC_STAT	Gathers information about the shared memory segment and places it in the structure pointed to by buf. This command requires a read permission to the shared memory segment.
IPC_SET	Sets the value of the shm_perm.uid, shm_perm.gid, and shm_perm. mode fields in the structure associated with shmid. The values are taken from the corresponding fields in the structure pointed to by buf. This operation can only be executed by the super-user or a process that has an effective user id equal to either shm_perm.cuid or shm_perm.uid in the data structure associated with the shared memory segment.
IPC_RMID	Removes the shared memory segment specified by shmid and destroys the data associated with it. Only the super-user or a process with an effective uid equal to the shm_perm.cuid or shm_perm.uid values in the data structure associated with the queue can do this.
IPC_INFO	Returns the information about the shared memory limits and parameters in the structure pointed by buf.
SHM_INFO	Returns an shm_info structure containing information about the consumed system resources by the shared memory.

Table 2-8 provides the description of function arguments.

Table 2-8. *Function arguments*

Function Arguments	Description
shmid	This is the identifier of the shared memory segment returned by the shmget() system call.
cmd	This is the command to perform the required control operation on the shared memory segment. It can take any value listed in Table 2-7.
buf	This is a pointer to the shared memory structure "shmid_ds". This value is used for either the set or the get as per cmd.

Table 2-9 provides the description of error codes in case of failure.

Table 2-9. *Errors*

Error Code	Description
EACCES	The command is IPC_STAT, and the caller has no read permission for this shared memory segment.
EFAULT	buf specified an invalid address.
EINVAL	shmid is not a valid shared memory segment.
EPERM	cmd is equal to IPC_SET or IPC_RMID, and the caller is not the super-user, nor does the effective uid match either the shm_perm. uid or shm_perm.cuid fields of the data structure associated with the shared memory segment. An attempt is made to increase the value of shm_qbytes through IPC_SET, but the caller is not the super-user.

Implementing IPC Using Shared Memory

To keep our focus on the IPC concepts and remove distractions which might arise due to a full-fledged Cocoa app, we will keep the implementation simple to understand. And to achieve this, we will create two C++ console apps to act like a server and a client, respectively.

The server app will write a string into the shared memory, and the client app will read this string from the same memory segment.

We will use the wait and monitoring mechanism to keep the server process alive till the client process reads the shared memory and overwrite it to make the server know that the process is complete.

As discussed in earlier sections of this chapter also, the server process should start earlier than the client process.

In the next sections, we will go through the code involved in the creation of server and client processes to implement IPC through shared memory.

Implementing Server Process

First, we will look into implementing a server process for the IPC. This process will write data in the shared memory for the client process to consume the data.

This process will be responsible for creating the shared memory segment and will act like a parent process for the client process.

To create a console application, open Xcode and create a new project as shown in Figure 2-2.

Figure 2-2. *Create a project*

From the project templates, choose "Command Line Tool" under the macOS tab as shown in Figure 2-3.

Figure 2-3. *Create a Command Line Tool*

As discussed, we will choose the Command Line Tool template to keep the app simple and just focus on IPC using shared memory.

Next, we will choose project configurations like the project name, language, organization identifier, and so on.

At this point, we will not assign any development team in the project configuration as this is just a sample app. We will need a development team during the actual project development to deploy it to a client machine.

Project configurations for the sample server app are shown in Figure 2-4.

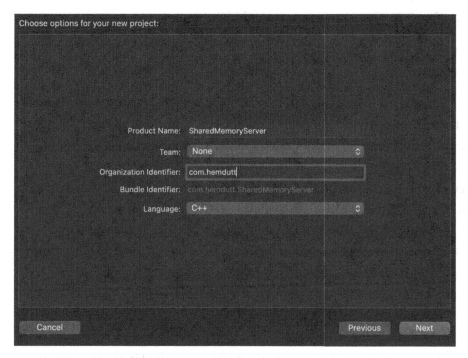

Figure 2-4. *Create a C++ project*

Save the project at an appropriate location, and let's look at the server implementation now.

Open the Xcode project, and in main.cpp, add the code from Listing 2-7.

Listing 2-7. Includes

```
#include <iostream>
#include <sys/types.h>
#include <sys/ipc.h>
#include <sys/shm.h>
#include <stdio.h>
#include <unistd.h>
```

Create constants as shown in Listing 2-8.

Listing 2-8. Constants (explained in Table 2-1)

```
#define PAGE_SIZE      27
#define KEY                   1097
```

It's time to write a method to create and get a shared memory segment (Listing 2-9). This method will create the segment using **shmget**() which returns the identifier of the shared memory segment associated with the value of the argument key. A new shared memory segment, with size equal to the value of the *size* argument passed in function rounded up to a multiple of PAGE_SIZE.

Also, this method will attach the segment to the data space using **shmat**() which attaches the shared memory segment identified by **shmid** to the address space of the calling process. The attaching address is specified by shmaddr with one of the following criteria:

If **shmaddr** is NULL, the system chooses a suitable (unused) address at which to attach the segment.

If shmaddr isn't NULL and SHM_RND is specified in shmflg, the attach occurs at the address equal to shmaddr rounded down to the nearest multiple of SHMLBA. Otherwise, shmaddr must be a page-aligned address at which the attach occurs.

Listing 2-9. getSharedMemorySpace()

```
void getSharedMemorySpace(char** sharedMemSpace)
{
    int sharedMemId;
    key_t key;
    //Name shared memory segment
    key = KEY;
    //create a shared memory segment
if ((sharedMemId = shmget(key, PAGE_SIZE, IPC_CREAT | 0666)) < 0)
```

```
{
    perror("Error in creating shared memory
    segment in function shmget");
  //Exit in case of error
    exit(1);
}
//attach shared memory segment to data space
if ((*sharedMemSpace = (char*)shmat(sharedMemId, NULL, 0))
== (char *)(-1))
{
    perror("Error in attaching segment to data space in
    function shmat");
  //Exit in case of error
    exit(1);
}
}
```

In the **main()** function (Listing 2-10), we will consume the function we defined in Listing 2-9. Here, we will create a string and will write that string in shared memory for the client app to consume.

To keep things simple, so that we can focus on the concept of IPC, we will use the **wait** and **monitoring** mechanism to keep the server app running till it gets an update in shared memory from the client app.

Listing 2-10. main()

```
int main(int argc, const char * argv[])
{
    // Execution of process starts here...
    char character;
    char *sharedMemSpace, *string;

    // Create and attach shared memory for the server process
```

```
getSharedMemorySpace(&sharedMemSpace);
string = sharedMemSpace;

//Create string to be shared
//It will be a simple alphabetic string created by
  concatenating the alphabets in sequence.
for (character = 'a'; character <= 'z'; ++character)
{
    *string++ = character;
}

*string = NULL;

//wait until the client proces changes the first character of
  our memory to '*', indicating that it has read what we put
  there.
while (*sharedMemSpace != '*')
{
    sleep(1);
}

return 0;
}
```

Next, we will go through the code for the client process.

Implementing Client Process

It's time to look into implementing a client process for the IPC. This process will read data from the shared memory written by the client process.

This is the consumer process, and after reading the data, it will update the shared memory segment so that the client process gets to know that the process is complete.

The initial steps to create a C++ console app for the client process are the same as shown in Figures 2-2 through 2-4. We will name this project "SharedMemoryClient."

Open the Xcode project, and in main.cpp, add the code from Listing 2-11.

Listing 2-11. Includes

```
#include <iostream>
#include <sys/types.h>
#include <sys/ipc.h>
#include <sys/shm.h>
#include <stdio.h>
#include <unistd.h>
```

Create constants as shown in Listing 2-12. These should match with the server process.

Listing 2-12. Constants

```
#define PAGE_SIZE    27
#define KEY                1097
```

It's time to write a method to get a shared memory segment (Listing 2-13). This method will create the segment using **shmget**() which returns the identifier of the shared memory segment associated with the value of the argument key.

Also, this method will attach the segment to the data space using **shmat**() which attaches the shared memory segment identified by **shmid** to the address space of the client process.

29

Listing 2-13. getSharedMemorySpace()

```
void getSharedMemorySpace(char** sharedMemSpace)
{
    int sharedMemId;
    key_t key;

    //program need to get the segment named KEY, created by the
      server.
    key = KEY;

    //Locate the segment.
    if ((sharedMemId = shmget(key, PAGE_SIZE, 0666)) < 0)
    {
        perror("Error in locating the segment in function shmget");
        exit(1);
    }

//Attach the segment to data space.
        if ((*sharedMemSpace = (char*)shmat(sharedMemId, NULL,
        0)) == (char *) -1)
    {
        perror("Error in attaching segment to data space in
        function shmat");
        exit(1);
    }
}
```

In the **main**() function (Listing 2-14), we will consume the function we defined in Listing 2-13. Here, we will read the string that was written by the server app into the shared memory segment and will update that string in shared memory for the server app to know that the process has completed.

Listing 2-14. main()

```
int main(int argc, const char * argv[])
{
    // Execution for the process code start here...
    char *sharedMemSpace;
    char *string;

    //Get sharedMemorySpace
    getSharedMemorySpace(&sharedMemSpace);

    //Now read what the server put in the memory.
    for (string = sharedMemSpace; *string != 0; ++string)
    {
      putchar(*string);
    }
    putchar('\n');

    //Finally, change the first character of the segment to
      '*', indicating program has read the segment.
    *sharedMemSpace = '*';

    return 0;
}
```

Run the server process first and then the client process and observe the results of the IPC. Next, we will discuss the scenarios where this IPC technique is useful and the pros and cons of this approach.

Pros and Cons of IPC Using Shared Memory

As discussed in earlier sections of this chapter, with respect to pipes or named pipes, IPC using shared memory is fast. In the case of pipes, a total of four copies of data are required, that is, two reads and two writes. On the contrary, with shared memory, the information is merely copied twice—from the input source into shared memory and from shared memory to the output.

But as any other technology, this technique also has its downside. The major downside is that it is very difficult to coordinate changes between server and client apps in the shared memory area. The client process does not get notified that a new data is available in the shared memory.

This technique needs to be implemented always with a synchronization mechanism between server and client apps.

Also, as discussed earlier, the server process and client process have a parent-child relationship, and so the server process should always start first, followed by the client process.

While implementing this technique for IPC, we also need to consider bounded buffer and unbounded buffer problems. Whether we go for a bounded buffer or unbounded buffer will depend on the case-by-case basis of the requirement. We will discuss both of these problems in detail in the next section.

Real-World Scenarios for IPC Using Shared Memory

In the real world, IPC by shared memory is used to transfer images between the application and the X server on Unix systems and inside the IStream object returned by CoMarshalInterThreadInterfaceInStream in the COM libraries on Windows OS. The classic example of using IPC using shared memory is the producer-consumer scenario where one process produces data to be consumed by another process.

In this case, the two participating processes share a common space in memory known as a buffer where the data produced by the producer is stored and from which the consumer consumes the data as shown in Figure 2-5.

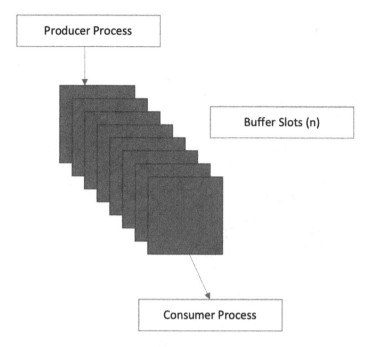

Figure 2-5. *Producer-consumer scenario*

The problem though is to make sure that the producer won't try to add data into the already full buffer, thus making the process crash or overwrite the previous data, and also make sure that the consumer won't try to remove data from an empty buffer, causing a crash of the process.

The solution lies into implementing a synchronization between producer and consumer processes. For the producer, there are two approaches, either go to sleep (Figure 2-6) or discard data if the buffer is full. When the consumer removes an item from the buffer, the producer will start putting the data into the buffer again.

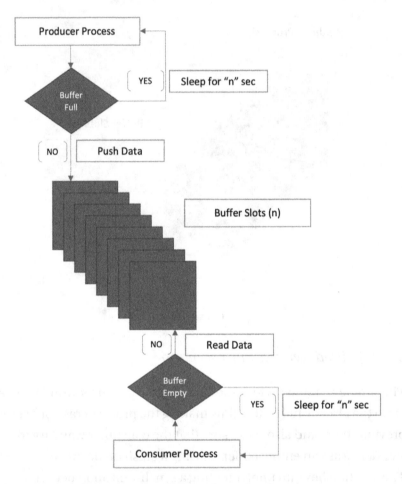

Figure 2-6. *Producer-consumer synchronization*

Similarly, the consumer can go to sleep (Figure 2-6) if it finds the buffer is empty. As the producer puts data into the buffer, the consumer can start consuming it.

This is one way of implementing and achieving a synchronization in IPC through shared memory. There are other multiple synchronization mechanisms available which can be used in this scenario like semaphores, monitors, mutex, and so on.

Summary

In this chapter, we discussed all about IPC using shared memory starting from understanding system calls and then implementing server and client processes using shared memory. During the course of this chapter, we touched upon all the technical aspects involved while implementing shared memory for IPC and gained insight to implement these concepts on real-world problems. In this chapter, we also touched upon the pros and cons of IPC using shared memory and also some of the real-world problems which got resolved using shared memory. Next up is IPC using Mach ports. Stay tuned!

CHAPTER 3

IPC Through Mach Ports

As discussed briefly in the first chapter, Mach ports are the fundamental services and primitives of the macOS kernel and are based on Mach 3.0 which was originally conceived as a simple, extensible, communications microkernel.

It is capable of running as a stand-alone kernel, with other traditional operating system services like I/O, file systems, and networking stacks running as user-mode servers.

These are conceptually similar to Unix pipes, sockets, or message queues. Mach ports are lightweight and powerful, but the downside is that these are poorly documented, making it difficult to implement IPC using Mach ports.

Introduction to Mach

In macOS, Mach and other kernel components are linked into a single kernel address space. This is primarily to enhance performance because it is very much faster to make a direct call between linked components than to send messages or do RPC between separate tasks.

This provides a modular structure which is more robust and extensible than a monolithic kernel and that too without the performance dip of a pure microkernel.

© Hem Dutt 2021
H. Dutt, *Interprocess Communication with macOS*,
https://doi.org/10.1007/978-1-4842-7045-5_3

In macOS, Mach is not principally a communication hub between clients and servers. Its value consists of its abstractions, extensibility, and flexibility.

All interprocess communication ultimately relies on Mach kernel APIs. Apart from IPC, Mach provides

- Object-based APIs with communication channels, for example, ports as object references

- Support for preemptively scheduled threads and SMP

- Support for the scheduling framework

- Support for IPC primitives, including messaging, RPC, synchronization, and notification

- Support for shared memory regions, large virtual address spaces, and memory objects backed by a persistent store

- Security and resource management as a fundamental principle of design

Mach provides a set of abstractions which are designed to be simple and powerful. The following are the kernel abstractions:

- **Tasks**: A task is the unit of resource ownership.

- **Threads**: A thread is the unit of CPU execution within a task.

- **Address space**: In combination with memory managers, Mach implements a sparse virtual address space and shared memory.

- **Memory objects**: Memory objects are internal units of memory management. These are representations of persistent data that may be mapped into address spaces.

- **Ports**: Secure, simplex communication channels, accessible only through port rights.

- **IPC**: Provides message queues, remote procedure calls, notifications, semaphores, and lock sets.

- **Time**: Provides clocks, timers, and waiting.

Tasks and Threads

A task is the unit of resource ownership. Each task consists of a port right namespace, a virtual address space, and one or more threads.

Threads are the units of CPU execution within a task.

macOS processes and POSIX threads also known as pthreads are implemented on top of Mach tasks and threads, respectively. A thread is a point of control flow in a task, whereas a task exists to provide resources for the threads it contains. This differentiation is made to provide parallelism and resource sharing.

A thread has access to all of the elements of the containing task. It executes in parallel (possibly) with other threads or with threads within the same task. A thread has minimal state information for low overhead.

A task on the other hand is a collection of system resources. These resources, except for the address space, are referenced by ports. These resources may be shared with other tasks based on the rights to the ports.

A task contains a number of threads and provides a large but potentially sparse address space, referenced by a virtual address. Parts of this space may be shared through inheritance or external memory management.

A task has no life span of its own; only threads execute instructions. When it is said that "task A performs B," it means that a thread contained within task A performed action B.

A task is an expensive entity. It exists as a collection of resources. All of the threads within a task share everything. Two tasks share nothing without an explicit action, and some resources such as port receive rights cannot be shared between two tasks at all.

On the other hand, a thread is a lightweight entity. It is inexpensive to create a thread and has low overhead to operate. This is because a thread has little state information. Its owner task carries the burden of resource management. On a multiprocessor computer, it is possible for multiple threads in a task to execute in parallel. Even when parallelism is not the goal, multiple threads do have an advantage that each thread can use a synchronous programming style, instead of attempting asynchronous programming with a single thread attempting to provide multiple services.

A thread is the basic computational entity. It belongs strictly to one and only one task that defines its virtual address space. To affect the structure of the address space or to reference any resource other than the address space, the thread must execute a special "trap instruction" that will cause the kernel to execute operations on behalf of the thread or to send a message to some agent on behalf of the thread. In general, these "trap instructions" manipulate the resources associated with the task containing the thread. Requests can be made of the kernel to manipulate these entities, that is, to create them, delete them, and affect their state.

Mach provides a flexible framework for thread scheduling policies. For real-time performance, macOS also provides time constraint scheduling. This scheduling allows us to specify that the thread must get a certain time quantum within a certain period of time.

Ports

Only except the task's virtual address space, all other Mach resources are accessed through ports. A port is an endpoint of a unidirectional communication channel between a client process and a server process. If a two-way communication is to be provided to such a service request, a second port must be used.

The resource accessed by the port, referred to as an object, and named by a port mostly has a single receiver and potentially multiple senders. This means there is only one receiver port and at least one sending port.

The service which needs to be provided by an object is determined by the manager which receives the request sent to the object. The kernel is the receiver for ports associated with kernel-provided objects, and the receiver for ports associated with task-provided objects is the task providing those objects.

For ports that name task-provided objects, it is possible to change the receiver of requests for that port to a different task by (say) passing the port to that task in a message. A single task may have multiple ports. Any given entity can have multiple ports representing it, implying different sets of permissible operations. For example, many objects may have a name port and a control port known as a privileged port. Access to the control port allows the object to be manipulated, whereas access to the name port simply names the object so that you can obtain information about it or perform other non-privileged operations against it.

Tasks have permissions known as port rights to access ports in certain ways, that is, send, receive, or send-once. A port can be accessed only through a right. Ports are generally used to grant clients access to objects within Mach. The right to send to the object's IPC port denotes the right to manipulate the object in certain ways. A port right ownership as such is the fundamental security mechanism within Mach. Having a right to an object means to have a capability to access or manipulate that object.

Port rights can be copied or moved between tasks via IPC. Doing so passes capabilities to some object or server.

A port set is one type of object referred to by a port. It is defined as a set of port rights that can be treated as a single unit when receiving a message or event from any of the members of the set. Port sets permit one thread to wait on a number of messages and event sources.

macOS supports additional types of communication channels along with a queue of messages, and these new types of IPC object are also represented by ports and port rights.

Ports and port rights do not have system-wide names to allow arbitrary ports or rights to be manipulated directly. Ports can be manipulated only by a task and that too if the task has a port right in its port namespace. A port right is specified by a port name which is an integer index into a 32-bit port namespace. Each task has a single port namespace associated with it.

Tasks acquire port rights when another task explicitly inserts them into its namespace, when they receive rights in messages, by creating objects that return a right to the object.

IPC with Mach

Communication between different tasks is an important element of the Mach architecture. Mach supports a client-server system architecture in which client tasks access services by making requests to server tasks through messages sent over a communication channel.

The endpoints of these communication channels in Mach are called ports, and port rights denote permissions to use the channel. The forms of IPC provided by Mach include

- Message queues

- Semaphores

- Notifications

- Lock sets

- Remote procedure calls (RPCs)

The operations permissible on the port and how data transfer will happen are determined by the type of the IPC object denoted by the port.

There are two fundamentally different Mach APIs available for the raw manipulation of a port, that is, the mach_ipc family and the mach_msg family. Both families may be used with any IPC object; however, the mach_ipc calls are preferred where we do not need to support legacy code because these maintain state information where appropriate in order to support the perception of a transaction. On the other hand, the mach_msg calls are supported for legacy code but are now deprecated and they are stateless.

IPC Transactions and Event Dispatching

When a process calls mach_ipc_dispatch, it repeatedly processes events coming in on the registered port set. These events could be an argument block from an RPC object, a lock object being taken by the same process, a notification or semaphore, or a message coming in from a traditional message queue.

These events are handled through callouts from mach_msg_dispatch. Some events denote a transaction during the lifetime of the callout. In the case of a lock, the state is the ownership of the lock, and when the callout returns, the lock is released. In the case of remote procedure calls, the state is the client process identity, the argument block, and the reply port. When the callout returns, the reply is sent.

When the callout returns, the transaction is completed, and the process waits for the next event. The mach_ipc_dispatch is intended to support work loops.

Message Queues

Originally, the IPC in Mach was through the message queue only. The receive right for a port denoting a message queue can only be held by one task. This task is also allowed to receive messages from the port queue. Multiple tasks can hold rights to the port that allow them to send messages into the queue.

43

A task communicates with another task after building a data structure that contains a set of data elements. Then it performs a message-send operation on a port for which it holds send rights. At some later time, the task with receive rights to that port will perform a message-receive operation.

A message may consist of some or all of the following:

- Pure data

- Copies of memory ranges

- Port rights

- Kernel implicit attributes, such as the sender's security token

The message transfer is an asynchronous operation. The message is logically copied into the receiving task. Multiple processes within the receiving task can attempt to receive messages from a given port, but only one process can receive any given message.

Semaphores

Semaphore IPC objects support wait, post, and post all operations. These are counting semaphores, that is, posts are saved if there is no process currently waiting in that semaphore's wait queue. A post all operation wakes up all the currently waiting threads.

Notifications

Similar to semaphores, notification objects also support post and wait operations, but with the addition of a state field. The state is a fixed-size, fixed-format field that is defined at the time when the notification object is created. Each post updates the state field, and there is a single state that is overwritten by each post.

Locks

A lock is an object that provides mutually exclusive access to a critical section. The primary interfaces to locks are transaction oriented. During the transaction, the process holds the lock. Upon returning from the transaction, the lock is released.

Remote Procedure Call (RPC) Objects

As the name indicates, an RPC object is for facilitating and optimizing remote procedure calls. The primary interfaces to RPC objects are transaction oriented.

On the creation of an RPC object, a set of argument block formats is defined. When an RPC is made by a client process, it creates a message in one of the predefined formats, and it gets queued on the object. Eventually, a message is passed to the server process. When the server process returns from the transaction, the response is returned to the sender.

Implementing IPC Using Mach Ports (Low-Level APIs)

To keep our focus on the IPC concepts and remove distractions which might arise due to a full-fledged Cocoa app, we will keep the implementation simple to understand. And to achieve this, we will create two C++ console apps to act like a server and a client, respectively.

The client app will open a port for reading messages on that port, and the server app will write messages to the same port.

The server process will terminate after sending a message to the client's port.

In the next sections, we will go through the code involved in the creation of server and client processes to implement IPC through Mach ports.

Implementing Server Process

First, we will look into implementing a server process for the IPC. This process will write data to a port for the client process to consume the data.

This process will be responsible for creating the message and writing to the port.

To create a console application, open Xcode and create a new project as shown in Figures 2-2 and 2-3.

We will name this project "MachPortsServer".

Open the Xcode project, and in main.cpp, add includes from Listing 3-1.

Listing 3-1. Includes

```
#include <iostream>
#include <stdio.h>
#include <mach/mach.h>
#include <servers/bootstrap.h>
```

Create a message structure as follows. This must match with the client process. This structure will provide a template for messages sent by the server and received and parsed by the client process.

In the absence of a template, it will be impossible for the client process to comprehend the message sent by the server process.

The message structure in Listing 3-2 acts like a protocol between the server and the client process to which both should adhere.

Listing 3-2. Message structure

```
struct Message
{
    mach_msg_header_t header;
    char hello_text[10];
    int sample_number;
    mach_msg_trailer_t trailer;
};
```

We will write a function to get a port for a particular service name (Listing 3-3). The service name is provided by the client process, and the same service name must be used by the server process to send a message to the port.

Listing 3-3. Get a port for a service

```
mach_port_t getMachPortForServiceName(name_t serviceName)
{
    mach_port_t port;
    kern_return_t kr = bootstrap_look_up(bootstrap_port,
    serviceName, &port);
    if (kr != KERN_SUCCESS)
    {
        printf("bootstrap_look_up() failed with code 0x%x\n", kr);
    }
    else
    {
        printf("bootstrap_look_up() returned port right name
        %d\n", port);
    }

    return port;
}
```

Now, we will create a message in main() (Listing 3-4) that needs to be sent from the server process to the client process. The message will be based on the template structure provided in Listing 3-2.

Listing 3-4. Message

```
// Construct the message.
struct {
    mach_msg_header_t header;
    char hello_text[10];
    int sample_number;
} message;

message.header.msgh_bits = MACH_MSGH_BITS(MACH_MSG_TYPE_COPY_
SEND, 0);
message.header.msgh_remote_port = port;
message.header.msgh_local_port = MACH_PORT_NULL;

strncpy(message.hello_text, "Hello", sizeof(message.hello_
text));
message.sample_number = 100;
```

Next, we will write a code in Main() to actually send the message created in Listing 3-4 on a client port. This is where IPC will happen. To do so, we will create an object of type **mach_msg** with the message object and other required configurations as presented in Listing 3-5.

Listing 3-5. Send a message

```
//Send message
kern_return_t kr;
kr = mach_msg(
    &message.header,   // Same as (mach_msg_header_t *) &message.
    MACH_SEND_MSG,     // Options. We're sending a message.
    sizeof(message),   // Size of the message being sent.
```

```
    0,                   // Size of the buffer for receiving.
    MACH_PORT_NULL,     // A port to receive a message on, if
                           receiving.
    MACH_MSG_TIMEOUT_NONE,
    MACH_PORT_NULL      // Port for the kernel to send
                           notifications about this message to.
);
if (kr != KERN_SUCCESS)
{
    printf("mach_msg() failed with code 0x%x\n", kr);
}
else
{
    printf("Sent a message\n");
}
```

At last, **main()** will look like Listing 3-6.

Listing 3-6. Start the server process

```
int main(int argc, const char * argv[])
{
    // Lookup the receiver port using the bootstrap server.
    mach_port_t port = getMachPortForServiceName((char*)
    "org.hemdutt.macportexample");
    if (port == 0)
    {
        //Failed in getting port
        return 1;
    }
    // Construct the message.
    struct {
        mach_msg_header_t header;
```

```
        char hello_text[10];
        int sample_number;
    } message;

    message.header.msgh_bits = MACH_MSGH_BITS(MACH_MSG_TYPE_
    COPY_SEND, 0);
    message.header.msgh_remote_port = port;
    message.header.msgh_local_port = MACH_PORT_NULL;

    strncpy(message.hello_text, "Hello", sizeof(message.hello_
    text));
    message.sample_number = 100;

    //Send message
    kern_return_t kr;
    kr = mach_msg(
        &message.header,   // Same as (mach_msg_header_t *)
        &message.
        MACH_SEND_MSG,     // Options. We're sending a message.
        sizeof(message),   // Size of the message being sent.
        0,                 // Size of the buffer for receiving.
        MACH_PORT_NULL,    // A port to receive a message on, if
                                  receiving.
        MACH_MSG_TIMEOUT_NONE,
        MACH_PORT_NULL     // Port for the kernel to send
                                  notifications about this message to.
    );
    if (kr != KERN_SUCCESS)
    {
        printf("mach_msg() failed with code 0x%x\n", kr);
    }
```

```
else
{
    printf("Sent a message\n");
}

return 0;
}
```

Implementing Client Process

Now, we will look into implementing the client process for the IPC. This process will open a port for the server process to send the data. The client process will listen to this port for any message coming from the server process.

To create a console application, open Xcode and create a new project as shown in Figures 2-2 and 2-3.

We will name this project "MachPortsClient".

Open the Xcode project, and in main.cpp, add the includes in Listing 3-7.

Listing 3-7. Includes

```
#include <iostream>
#include <stdio.h>
#include <mach/mach.h>
#include <servers/bootstrap.h>
```

Create a message structure as described in Listing 3-2. This structure will provide a template for messages sent by the server and received and parsed by the client process. A message structure on the client process must always match with the server process to make IPC successful. Next, we will write a function to create and get a port for listening for the message from the server.

We will create a port using the mach_port_allocate() function with MACH_PORT_RIGHT_RECEIVE (Listing 3-8).

Listing 3-8. Create and get a port for listening for a message

```
mach_port_t getMachPort()
{
    mach_port_t port;
    kern_return_t kr = mach_port_allocate(mach_task_self(),
    MACH_PORT_RIGHT_RECEIVE, &port);
    if (kr != KERN_SUCCESS)
    {
        printf("mach_port_allocate() failed with code 0x%x\n", kr);
    }
    else
    {
        printf("mach_port_allocate() created port right name
        %d\n", port);
    }

    return port;
}
```

Next, we will give "send rights" on the port using mach_port_insert_ right() and MACH_MSG_TYPE_MAKE_SEND (Listing 3-9).

Listing 3-9. Give send rights

```
kern_return_t giveSendRightsOnPort(mach_port_t port)
{
    kern_return_t kr = mach_port_insert_right(mach_task_self(),
    port, port, MACH_MSG_TYPE_MAKE_SEND);
    if (kr != KERN_SUCCESS)
    {
```

```
        printf("mach_port_insert_right() failed with code
        0x%x\n", kr);
    }
    else
    {
        printf("mach_port_insert_right() inserted a send
        right\n");
    }

    return kr;
}
```

Now, we will send "send rights" to the **Bootstrap Server** so that the port can be looked up by other processes. We will register the service name through which the server process will identify the port (Listing 3-10).

Listing 3-10. Register a service name

```
kern_return_t sendSendRightsToBootstrapServer(mach_port_t port ,
name_t serviceName)
{
    kern_return_t kr = bootstrap_register(bootstrap_port,
    serviceName, port);
    if (kr != KERN_SUCCESS)
    {
        printf("bootstrap_register() failed with code 0x%x\n", kr);
    }
    else
    {
        printf("bootstrap_register()'ed our port\n");
    }

    return kr;
}
```

Next, we will start listening on this port to capture any message from the server process and further parse and process the message. For the sample process, we will send a text and a number from the server process on this port to be captured and printed by the client process (Listing 3-11).

Listing 3-11. Start listening on the port

```
void startListeningMessageOnPort(mach_port_t port)
{
    // Wait for a message.
    Message message;
    kern_return_t kr = mach_msg(
        &message.header, // Same as (mach_msg_header_t *)
                                    &message.
        MACH_RCV_MSG,    // Options. We're receiving a message.
        0,               // Size of the message being sent, if
                            sending.
        sizeof(message), // Size of the buffer for receiving.
        port,            // The port to receive a message on.
                            MACH_MSG_TIMEOUT_NONE,
        MACH_PORT_NULL   // Port for the kernel to send
                            notifications about this message to.
    );
    if (kr != KERN_SUCCESS)
    {
        printf("mach_msg() failed with code 0x%x\n", kr);
    }
    printf("Received message\n");
    message.hello_text[9] = 0;
    printf("Text: %s, Number: %d\n", message.hello_text,
    message.sample_number);
}
```

At last, we will invoke these functions in **Main()** to execute the client process (Listing 3-12).

Listing 3-12. Start the client process

```
int main(int argc, const char * argv[]) {
    // Create a new port.
    mach_port_t port = getMachPort();
    // Give send right to this port, in addition to the receive
       right.
    if (giveSendRightsOnPort(port) != KERN_SUCCESS)
    {
        return 1;
    }

    // Send the send right to the bootstrap server, so that it
       can be looked up by other processes.
    if (sendSendRightsToBootstrapServer(port, (char*)"org.
    hemdutt.macportexample") != KERN_SUCCESS)
    {
        return 1;
    }

    startListeningMessageOnPort(port);

    return 0;
}
```

Time to Run the Code!

Run the client process first. The client process will create the port and open the port for other processes to send messages. Client logs are mentioned in Listing 3-13.

Listing 3-13. Client logs at launch

```
mach_port_allocate() created port right name 4867
mach_port_insert_right() inserted a send right
bootstrap_register()'ed our port
```

Next, run the server process and observe the results of the IPC in the console. Server logs are mentioned in Listing 3-14.

Listing 3-14. Server logs after sending a message

```
bootstrap_look_up() returned port right name 4611
Sent a message
Program ended with exit code: 0
```

The client process on receiving the message from the server will print the logs in the console (Listing 3-15).

Listing 3-15. Client logs after receiving a message

```
Recieved message
Text: Hello, Number: 100
Program ended with exit code: 0
```

Next, we will discuss this IPC technique with higher level api's in a Cocoa project.

Implementing IPC Using Mach Ports (High-Level APIs)

Core Foundation and Foundation frameworks provide higher-level APIs for Mach ports. NSMachPort is a wrapper on top of the kernel APIs that can be used as a run loop source.

Now we will look into the implementation of IPC using Mach ports using high-level NSMachPort and associated classes.

Implementing Server Process

First, we will look into implementing the server process for the IPC. This process will write data to a port for the client process to consume the data.

This process will be responsible for creating the message and writing to the port.

To create a console application, open Xcode and create a new project as shown in Figures 2-2 and 2-3.

We will name this project "MachPortsServer-HighLevel". Add a new Cocoa class file named "MachPortServer" in the project as shown in Figures 3-1 and 3-2.

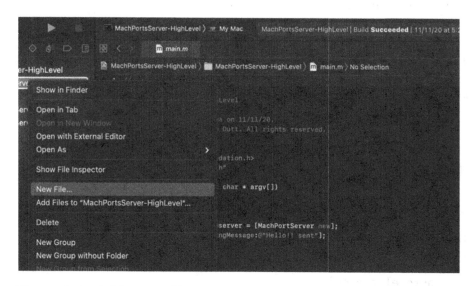

Figure 3-1. *Add a new file*

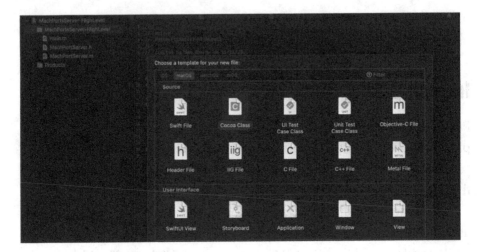

Figure 3-2. *Add a Cocoa class*

This will create two files named **MachPortServer.h** and
MachPortServer.m.

Next, we will add includes in main.m (Listing 3-16).

Listing 3-16. Includes in main.m

```
#import <Foundation/Foundation.h>
#import "MachPortServer.h"
```

Now is the time to initialize the MachPortServer class in main.m
(Listing 3-17).

Listing 3-17. Initialize MachPortServer in main.m

```
int main(int argc, const char * argv[])
{
    @autoreleasepool
    {
        MachPortServer *server = [MachPortServer new];
        [server sendStringMessage:@"Hello!! sent"];
    }
```

```
    return 0;
}
```

Time to look into the server class implementation now to send some data to the client process.

First, let's look at the MachPortServer.h class and add includes (Listing 3-18).

Listing 3-18. Includes in MachPortServer.h

```
#import <Foundation/Foundation.h>
```

MachPortServer will conform to NSPortDelegate to capture messages on the port (Listing 3-19).

Listing 3-19. MachPortServer class

```
@interface MachPortServer : NSObject<NSPortDelegate>
{
    BOOL _responseReceived;
}
- (void)sendStringMessage:(NSString *)string;
@end
```

Now we will write the implementation for the MachPortServer class in the MachPortServer.m file.

First, define the service name (Listing 3-20).

Listing 3-20. Includes in MachPortServer.m

```
#import "MachPortServer.h"
#define SERVICE_NAME @"org.hemdutt.example"
```

Write a function to get the service port (Listing 3-21).

Listing 3-21. Get a service port

```
- (NSPort *)getServicePort
{
    return [[NSMachBootstrapServer sharedInstance]
            portForName:SERVICE_NAME];
}
```

Implement a function to send a text message to the client app (Listing 3-22) on the service port obtained in Listing 3-21.

Listing 3-22. Send a text message to the service port

```
- (void)sendStringMessage:(NSString *)string
{
    NSData *data = [string dataUsingEncoding:NSUTF8String
    Encoding];

    NSPort *sendToPort = [self getServicePort];
    if (sendToPort == nil)
    {
        NSLog(@"Unable to connect to service port");
        return;
    }

    //Client Server in IPC terminology are interchangeable and
    based on which service is sending data and which service is
    receiving data.
    //We will create a receiver port as well for this service.
    NSPort *receivePort = [NSMachPort port];
    receivePort.delegate = self;

    NSRunLoop *runLoop = [NSRunLoop currentRunLoop];
    [runLoop addPort:receivePort forMode:NSDefaultRunLoopMode];
```

```
NSPortMessage *message = [[NSPortMessage alloc]
                          initWithSendPort:sendToPort
                          receivePort:receivePort
                          components:@[data]];
_responseReceived = NO;
NSDate *timeout = [NSDate dateWithTimeIntervalSinceNow:5.0];
if (![message sendBeforeDate:timeout]) {
    NSLog(@"Send failed");
}

while (!_responseReceived) {
    [runLoop runUntilDate:
     [NSDate dateWithTimeIntervalSinceNow:0.1]];
}
}
```

Next, we will implement a delegate function for NSPort to receive the response from the client and allow exit of the server process (Listing 3-23).

Listing 3-23. Implement a port delegate

```
- (void)handlePortMessage:(NSPortMessage *)message
{
    _responseReceived = YES;
}
```

Implementing Client Process

In this section, we will look into implementing the client process for the IPC. This process will open a port and listen for the data written by the server process.

To create a console application, open Xcode and create a new project as shown in Figures 2-2 and 2-3 in Chapter 2.

We will name this project "MachPortsClient-HighLevel". Add a new Cocoa class file named "MachPortClient" in the project as shown in Figures 3-1 and 3-2.

Add includes in the main.m file (Listing 3-24).

Listing 3-24. Includes in main.m

```
#import <Foundation/Foundation.h>
#import "MachPortClient.h"
```

Next, initialize the MachPortClient class in main.m (Listing 3-25).

Listing 3-25. Initialize MachPortClient in main.m

```
int main(int argc, const char * argv[])
{
    @autoreleasepool
    {
        MachPortClient *client = [MachPortClient new];
        [client initiate];
    }
    return 0;
}
```

Time to look into the client class implementation now to open the port and receive data from the server process.

First, let's look at the MachPortClient.h class and add includes (Listing 3-26).

Listing 3-26. Includes in MachPortClient.h

```
#import <Foundation/Foundation.h>
```

Similar to the MachPortServer class, MachPortClient will conform to NSPortDelegate to capture messages on the port (Listing 3-27).

Listing 3-27. MachPortClient class

```
@interface MachPortClient : NSObject<NSPortDelegate>

@property NSPort *port;
- (void)initiate;

@end
```

Now we will write the implementation for the MachPortClient class in the MachPortClient.m file.

First, define the service name (Listing 3-28).

Listing 3-28. Includes in MachPortClient.m

```
#import "MachPortClient.h"

#define SERVICE_NAME @"org.hemdutt.example"
```

Next, implement a function to open a port for receiving text messages from the server app (Listing 3-29).

Listing 3-29. Open a port

```
- (void)initiate
{
    self.port = [[NSMachBootstrapServer sharedInstance]
                  servicePortWithName:SERVICE_NAME];
    if (self.port == nil)
    {
        // This probably means another instance is running.
        NSLog(@"Unable to open server port.");
        return;
    }

    self.port.delegate = self;
```

```
    NSRunLoop *runLoop = [NSRunLoop currentRunLoop];
    [runLoop addPort:self.port forMode:NSDefaultRunLoopMode];
    [runLoop run];
}
```

At last, we will implement a delegate function for NSPort to receive the message from the server process and send a response to the server process (Listing 3-30).

Listing 3-30. Receive a message on the port and respond

```
- (void)handlePortMessage:(NSPortMessage *)message
{
    NSPort *responsePort = message.sendPort;
    if (responsePort != nil)
    {
        NSArray *components = message.components;
        if (components.count > 0)
        {
            NSString *data = [[NSString alloc]
                                    initWithData:components[0]
                                  encoding:NSUTF8StringEncoding];
            NSLog(@"Received data: \"%@\"", data);
        }
        NSPortMessage *response = [[NSPortMessage alloc]
                                    initWithSendPort:responsePort
                                    receivePort:nil
                                    components:message.components];
        response.msgid = message.msgid;
        NSDate *timeout = [NSDate dateWithTimeIntervalSinceNow:5.0];
        [response sendBeforeDate:timeout];
        NSLog(@"Sent feedback response");
    }
}
```

Time to Run the Code!

Similar to the low-level API example, run the client process first and then run the server process. After receiving a message from the server, the client process will send a feedback to the server and log the message listed in Listing 3-31.

Listing 3-31. Client logs

```
MachPortsClient-HighLevel[22477:1280368] Received data:
"Hello!! sent"
MachPortsClient-HighLevel[22477:1280368] Sent feedback response
```

This sums up the implementation of IPC using Mach ports. Next, we will discuss the scenarios where this IPC technique is useful and the pros and cons of this approach.

Pros and Cons of IPC Using Mach Ports

All IPC techniques at the end rely on the functionality provided by Mach kernel APIs. Mach ports are lightweight and powerful, and this is a major advantage, but the biggest disadvantage is that the APIs are poorly documented.

Fortunately, Core Foundation and Foundation frameworks provide higher-level APIs for Mach ports. NSMachPort is a wrapper on top of the kernel APIs that can be used as a run loop source, while NSMessagePort facilitates the synchronous communication between two ports.

NSMachPort allows for local communication only. A companion SocketPort class allows for both local and remote distributed object communication, but may be more expensive than NSMachPort for the local case.

Real-World Scenarios for IPC Using Mach Ports

Mach ports provide a lightweight and fast IPC mechanism, but it is not generally used for IPC between high-level applications. It's a low-level implementation of IPC, which makes the base for other IPC techniques available at a higher abstraction level.

Summary

In this chapter, we discussed all about IPC using Mach ports. Till now, we have discussed IPC between two local processes, that is, IPC between processes residing on the same machine. Next, we will dig deep into IPC using Sockets and IPC between processes residing on different machines.

CHAPTER 4

IPC Through Sockets

Most programs written using high-level network APIs are purely clients. At a lower level, however, the lines are blurry. In this chapter we will explore all these concepts and will create a IPC channel between a client and server application using Sockets.

Introduction to Socket Programming

Socket and stream programming can be divided into the following categories:

Packet-based communication programs: Operating on one packet at a time, listening for incoming packets, then sending packets in reply.

With packet-based communication, the only differences between clients and servers are the contents of the packets that each program sends and receives and what each program does with the data. The networking code itself is identical.

Stream-based client programs: Programs using TCP to send and receive data as two continuous streams of bytes, one in each direction.

With stream-based communication, clients and servers are more distinct. How clients and servers handle data is similar, but the way that the program initially constructs the communication channel is very different.

© Hem Dutt 2021
H. Dutt, *Interprocess Communication with macOS*,
https://doi.org/10.1007/978-1-4842-7045-5_4

The API you choose for socket-based connections depends on two factors:

1. Whether you are making a connection to another host or receiving a connection from another host

2. Whether you are using TCP or some other protocol

Here are some other factors to consider.

If you want to reuse and share your networking code among non-Apple platforms, you can use POSIX C networking APIs and continue to use networking code as is. If the process or application relies on the Core Foundation or Cocoa run loop, we will use the Core Foundation framework's CFStream API to integrate the POSIX networking code with the overall architecture on the main thread. Alternatively, if you're using Grand Central Dispatch (GCD), you can add a socket as a dispatch source.

If you want to use POSIX networking code, you should know that the POSIX networking API is not protocol agnostic, and you must handle differences between IPv4 and IPv6 yourself. It is a connect-by-IP API rather than a connect-by-name API, which means that you must do a lot of extra manipulations if you want to achieve the same initial connection performance and robustness that higher-level APIs give without any hassle.

Before we decide to reuse existing POSIX networking code, make sure to read the following link:

```
https://developer.apple.com/library/archive/documentation/
NetworkingInternetWeb/Conceptual/NetworkingOverview/
CommonPitfalls/CommonPitfalls.html#//apple_ref/doc/uid/
TP40010220-CH4-SW20
```

For daemons or services that listen to a port, or for non-TCP connections, use POSIX or Core Foundation (CFSocket) C networking APIs.

For client code in Objective-C or Swift, use Foundation networking APIs. The Foundation framework defines high-level classes for managing URL connections, socket streams, network services, and other networking tasks.

For client code in C, use Core Foundation C networking APIs. The Core Foundation framework and the CFNetwork framework are two of the primary C language frameworks in macOS. Together these frameworks define the functions and structures on which the Foundation networking classes are built.

The frameworks and APIs we use for an outgoing connection depend on what programming language we are using, on the type of connection (TCP, UDP), and on whether we are trying to create a shared module for multiple other (non-Mac, non-iOS) platforms.

If you are creating outgoing connections in Objective-C, use NSStream.

If you want to connect to a specific host, create a CFHost object and then use CFStreamCreatePairWithSocketToHost or CFStreamCreatePairWithSocketToCFHost to open a socket connected to that host and port and associate a pair of CFStream objects with it. Then you can cast these to an NSStream object.

To connect to a Bonjour service, we can also use the CFStreamCreatePairWithSocketToNetService method with a CFNetServiceRef object.

NSNetService requires an instance of NSHost. When you create an object, the lookup is performed synchronously, so you must not construct an NSHost object on your main application thread.

If you are creating outgoing connections in C, use CFStream.

If you are writing code which is not compatible with Objective-C, use the CFStream API. It integrates more easily with other Core Foundation APIs than CFSocket. You can use CFStreamCreatePairWithSocketToHost or CFStreamCreatePairWithSocketToCFHost for opening a socket connected to a given host and port and then associate a pair of CFStream objects with it.

You can also use the CFStreamCreatePairWithSocketToNetService function to attach to a Bonjour service.

If cross-platform portability is required, use POSIX calls.

If you are writing networking code exclusively for OS X, you should avoid POSIX networking calls, because they are cumbersome to work with as compared to higher-level APIs. However, if you are writing networking code that needs to be shared with other platforms, you can use the POSIX networking APIs so that you can use the same code everywhere on multiple platforms.

You should never use synchronous POSIX networking APIs on the main thread of a GUI application. If you employ synchronous networking calls in a GUI application, you need to do so on a separate thread.

The recommended way to establish a TCP connection to a remote host is through streams. Streams automatically handle many challenges that TCP connections present such as providing the ability to connect by a hostname.

Streams also are a more Cocoa-like networking interface than lower-level protocols, and they behave in a way that's largely compatible with the Cocoa file stream APIs.

If you know the DNS name or IP address of the remote host already, get Core Foundation read and write streams with the CFStreamCreatePairWithSocketToHost function.

You can also make use of the toll-free bridge between CFStream and NSStream to cast CFReadStreamRef and CFWriteStreamRef objects to NSInputStream and NSOutputStream objects.

If you discovered the host after browsing for network services with a CFNetServiceBrowser object, you must obtain input and output streams for the service with the CFStreamCreatePairWithSocketToNetService function.

After you've obtained your input and output streams, you must retain them immediately if you're not using automatic reference counting. You can then cast them to NSInputStream and NSOutputStream objects, set their delegate objects (conforming to the NSStreamDelegate protocol), schedule them on the current run loop, and call their open methods.

As discussed earlier, there are many Apple's network APIs we can use for networking, the older APIs are well documented, and many sample codes are available.

With Mac OS 10.14 onward, Apple provides the new Network framework which is less documented and fewer sample codes are available, but I found it to be very powerful to make server and client applications.

In this chapter, we'll specialize in this very framework, and I will explain the way to use the **Network framework** by creating a basic TCP server-client application.

The server will work as an echo server which can basically remit any message received from the client. The client then will allow us to send messages to the server and display the server response.

But before going further with the **Network framework**, let's start by reviewing some networking concepts.

We aren't aiming to go too deep into details, only a general overview of networking, so we are able to start from the identical base. Let's take the reference of the OSI model to grasp different layers involved in networking and where we are getting to work (Table 4-1).

Table 4-1. *OSI model*

Layer	Protocol Data Unit	Function
7. Application	Data	High-level APIs, including resource sharing, remote file access
6. Presentation	Data	Translation of data between a networking service and an application, including character encoding, data compression, and encryption/decryption
5. Session	Data	Managing communication sessions, i.e., continuous exchange of information in the form of multiple back-and-forth transmissions between two nodes
4. Transport	Segment and Datagram	Reliable transmission of data segments between points on a network, including segmentation, acknowledgment, and multiplexing
3. Network	Packet	Structuring and managing a multi-node network, including addressing, routing, and traffic control
2. Data link	Frame	Reliable transmission of data frames between two nodes connected by a physical layer
1. Physical	Bit, Symbol	Transmission and reception of raw bit streams over a physical medium

We are going to be working from layers four to seven (i.e., Transport to Application). We use all the lower layers, but we don't directly interface with them.

We will use Sockets to make connections between nodes (which are client and server applications in our example). And we are going to be using TCP as our transport protocol.

The reason why we used TCP in our example is that the most common transport protocols are TCP and UDP. Both of these provide the capability of sending datagrams, the key differences being in how they handle package loss and order.

TCP checks for package loss and also cares about the package order, whereas UDP is stateless. It does not concern itself with any package loss, and if it receives a package out of order, it'll just drop it.

Based on your application-specific requirement, you can select the one that works best for your case. For example:

If we are sending a document, we want all the data to be received and in order. Then, TCP will be our choice.

But, if we are in a call, we don't mind some loss. The conversation could lose some packages. There is a certain flexibility. In this case, use UDP.

There are more transport protocols available as well, but unless you are in a particular case, you are more likely to work with TCP or UDP.

Again, summarizing all we have discussed earlier about various networking API families provided by Apple, here is a list of major networking API families with a small description on when you would decide to use them (Table 4-2).

Table 4-2. *Networking API families provided by Apple*

API Family	Description
C POSIX (BSD) Sockets	Provides access to the lowest layer, i.e., to the Link layer. socket() creates an endpoint for communication and returns a file descriptor that refers to that endpoint. The file descriptor returned by a successful call will be the lowest-numbered file descriptor not currently open for the process. The domain argument specifies a communication domain. This selects the protocol family which will be used for communication. These families are defined in <sys/socket.h>. More information here: `https://man7.org/linux/man-pages/man2/socket.2.html`
CFNetwork	This is provided by the Core Foundation framework. **CFSocket**: Provides an abstraction on top of BSD Sockets integrating RunLoop support. A CFSocket can be created from a BSD Socket and can be added to your current RunLoop (CFRunLoopAddSource or CFSocketCreateRunLoopSource). If you are working only on Apple's environment and you need low-level sockets, you can consider CFSocket instead of directly using BSD sockets. **CFStream**: This allows you to stream data in and out of memory, files, and more important for our case, network via Sockets. It abstracts the Socket so we can read and write as if we were using a file descriptor. If you want to read data as is coming through the socket, then have a look at CFStreams. **Other APIs**: There are many other APIs like CFFTP, CFHTTP, CFHTTPAuthentication, CFHOST, CFNetServices, and CFNetDiagnostics provided by Core Foundation, but we won't be discussing those into much details.

(continued)

Table 4-2. (*continued*)

API Family	Description
NSStream	This API is available at the Cocoa level and based on the Core Foundation APIs. This Cocoa API is based on CFStream, and so you will find a lot of similarity. NSStream uses the delegate pattern for asynchronous tasks, whereas CFStream uses the callbacks to handle the asynchronous tasks. Also, because NSStream belongs to Objective-C, you can subclass it and build new classes that can be extended and fit to your needs. If you are in the Objective-C environment, use NSStream. **NSURLConnection**: It provides an abstraction over NSStream that gives us easier access to making requests to URLs using the most common protocols (HTTP, HTTPS, and FTP). This API has been deprecated by NSURLSession, so there is no real need to use it unless you need to keep compatibility for some weird edge case. **NSURLSession**: This API provides many new advantages from NSURLConnection; it allows us to download code without using a delegate, perform background downloads, and many more features. This API has been superseded by URLSession on Swift, so if you are using Swift, use URLSession.
Network	The Network framework is supported on Mac OS 10.14 onward and provides direct access to TLS, TCP, and UDP. If you need to work at the transport layer level, this should be your choice. The Network framework abstracts a lot of the boilerplate and setup required by the alternatives like CFSockets or raw sockets. It creates network connections to send and receive data using transport and security protocols. Continue to use URLSession, which is built upon this framework, for loading HTTP- and URL-based resources.

In our client and server implementation, we are going to be using the Network framework.

Implementing IPC Using Sockets (Network Framework)

We are going to create a server that echoes every message it receives and a client that can send commands and read the server response.

For this, we are going to use the Network framework because we don't want to only support common application protocols (like HTTP or FTP), but we also want our server to handle any custom protocol and that our client can send any message to any server.

We are going to build two command-line applications for better distinction between server and client processes.

Generally, an application can act as a server and a client both based on the context, and so code from both applications can be used to create a single application as well.

The server application will be listening on the port that we will specify, and the client will connect to the server and port that we will specify and want to connect to.

Implementing Server Process

First, we will create a command-line application using Xcode as shown in Figure 4-1.

Figure 4-1. *Create a command-line application*

Open Xcode, create a new project (File ➤ New ➤ Project), and select
macOS ➤ Command Line Tool.

We will name our socket-based server application as
"SocketsServerExample".

We are going to use the Swift language for the development of our
command-line application as shown in Figure 4-2.

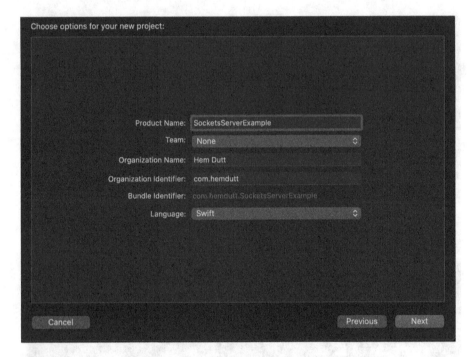

Figure 4-2. Use Swift for the command-line application

Before proceeding any further, add the Network framework in the project. Click "SocketsServerExample" ➤ TARGETS ➤ SocketsServerExample.

Under General tab ➤ Frameworks and Libraries, click the "+" button to add a Network framework as shown in Figure 4-3.

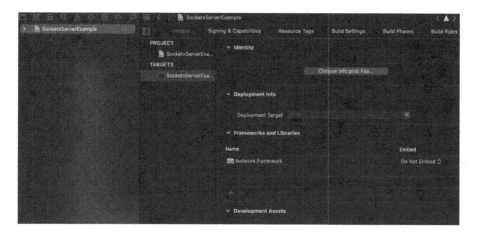

Figure 4-3. *Add a Network framework*

Now we are ready to write our code, and so let's start with the connection class. Create a new Swift file, and we will name this "ServerConnection.swift".

This is a wrapper class to wrap NWConnection, so it'll be easy to keep the Connection code separated and easier to understand.

Import the Network framework in the class (Listing 4-1).

Listing 4-1. Includes in ServerConnection

```
import Foundation
import Network
```

Add an OS version check over this class as the Network framework is only available on Mac OS 10.14 onward (Listing 4-2).

Listing 4-2. OS X version check

```
@available(macOS 10.14, *)
class ServerConnection
{

}
```

Next, we will declare some instance variables in the ServerConnection class (Listing 4-3).

Listing 4-3. Instance variables in ServerConnection

```
//The TCP package size
let ps = 65536

private static var nextId: Int = 0
let  connection: NWConnection
let id: Int

//Callback for did stop event
var didStopCallback: ((Error?) -> Void)? = nil
```

Next, we will write the initializers and start function for the ServerConnection class (Listing 4-4).

Listing 4-4. Initializer in ServerConnection

```
init(connection: NWConnection)
{
    self.connection = connection
    id = ServerConnection.nextId
    ServerConnection.nextId += 1
}

func start()
{
    print("connection with \(id) will start")
    connection.stateUpdateHandler = self.stateDidChange(to:)
    setupReceive()
    connection.start(queue: .main)
}
```

nextId represents an incremental counter for our connection ids, and so we are keeping track of it and increment it after each connection.

Every time we create a new connection, we assign the id and increment the counter.

The **NWConnection** class in the **Network** framework also defines a stateUpdateHandler to manage the state changes.

The function setupReceive (Listing 4-5) prepares the connection to receive data; we will look into this next.

Listing 4-5. setupReceive

```
private func setupReceive()
{
    connection.receive(minimumIncompleteLength: 1,
    maximumLength: ps) { (data, _, isComplete, error) in
        if let data = data, !data.isEmpty
        {
            let message = String(data: data, encoding: .utf8)
            print("connection \(self.id) did receive message: \
            (message ?? "nil")")
            self.send(data: data)
        }
        if isComplete
        {
            self.connectionDidEnd()
        }
        else if let error = error
        {
            self.connectionDidFail(error: error)
        }
        else
        {
```

```
        self.setupReceive()
    }
  }
}
```

setupReceive calls receive on NWConnection and passes a closure that will be called when data is received. In our case, we will send data back to the client as an echo after reading the data from the client.

Our implementation to handle the state change (stateDidChange) is really simple (Listing 4-6); it just displays what event is occurring.

Listing 4-6. stateDidChange

```
private func stateDidChange(to state: NWConnection.State)
{
    switch state
    {
    case .waiting(let error):
        connectionDidFail(error: error)
    case .ready:
        print("connection with \(id) ready")
    case .failed(let error):
        connectionDidFail(error: error)
    default:
        break
    }
}
```

Now we will implement a send function (Listing 4-7) which when invoked will send on our NWConnection object and passes a closure that will be called when the content is processed.

Listing 4-7. Send method

```
func send(data: Data)
{
    self.connection.send(content: data, completion:
    .contentProcessed( { error in
        if let error = error
        {
            self.connectionDidFail(error: error)
            return
        }
        print("connection \(self.id) did send data: \(data as
        NSData)")
    }))
}
```

Next, we will implement functions to capture connection did end and connection did fail events (Listings 4-8 and 4-9).

Listing 4-8. connectionDidEnd

```
private func connectionDidEnd()
{
    print("connection \(id) did end")
    stop(error: nil)
}
```

Listing 4-9. connectionDidFail

```
private func connectionDidFail(error: Error)
{
    print("connection \(id) did fail, error: \(error)")
    stop(error: error)
}
```

At last, we will write functions for stop connections (Listings 4-10 and 4-11).

Listing 4-10. Stop

```
func stop()
{
    print("connection \(id) will stop")
}
```

Listing 4-11. Stop with error

```
private func stop(error: Error?)
{
    connection.stateUpdateHandler = nil
    connection.cancel()
    if let didStopCallback = didStopCallback
    {
        self.didStopCallback = nil
        didStopCallback(error)
    }
}
```

Our server will listen for incoming connections, and once the connection is established, the server should append it to a list of active connections.

To handle the listening, we are going to use an NWListener object. The NWListener waits for connections and will call the newConnectionHandler function every time it gets a new connection.

We will see how Network framework objects rely on handler functions to manage events and changes in state.

Let's create our server interface by creating a new file **Server.swift**.

Import the Network framework in the class (Listing 4-12). We imported the Network framework to have access to NWListener, NWEndpoint, and NWConnection.

Listing 4-12. Includes in Server

```
import Foundation
import Network
```

Add an OS version check over this class as the Network framework is only available on Mac OS 10.14 onward (Listing 4-13).

Listing 4-13. OS X version check

```
@available(macOS 10.14, *)
class Server
{

}
```

Next, we will declare some instance variables in the Server class (Listing 4-14).

Listing 4-14. Instance variables in Server

```
private var port: NWEndpoint.Port?
private var listener: NWListener?

private var connections: [Int: ServerConnection] = [:]
```

Next, we will write the initializers and start function for the ServerConnection class (Listing 4-15).

Listing 4-15. Initializer in Server

```
init(port: UInt16)
{
    guard let endPoint =  NWEndpoint.Port(rawValue: port) else
    {
        return
    }
    self.port = endPoint
    do
    {
        listener = try NWListener(using: .tcp, on: self.port!)
    }
    catch let error
    {
        print(error.localizedDescription)
    }
}
```

Now we will create a start function (Listing 4-16) that will start the listening and handling of connections.

We will use the main queue to run our server code. But in the case of our client code, we will create a specific queue to handle the asynchronous connections.

Listing 4-16. Start Server

```
func start() throws
{
    if listener == nil
    {
        print("Server configuration not correct. can not
        start...")
```

```
        return
    }
    print("Server starting...")
    listener!.stateUpdateHandler = self.stateDidChange(to:)
    listener!.newConnectionHandler = self.
    didAccept(connection:)
    listener!.start(queue: .main)
}
```

We defined the handler functions for the listener.stateUpdateHandler and listener.newConnectionHandler. Now let's implement stateDidChange (Listing 4-17).

In case of failure, we will exit. For other cases, we are simply logging the state to be state conscious when the server is running.

Listing 4-17. stateDidChange

```
func stateDidChange(to state: NWListener.State)
{
    switch state
    {
    case .ready:
        print("Server ready.")
    case .cancelled:
        print("Operation Cancelled.")
    case .waiting(let error):
        print("Server waiting, reason: \(error.
        localizedDescription)")
    case .failed(let error):
        print("Server failure, error: \(error.
        localizedDescription)")
        exit(EXIT_FAILURE)
```

```
    default:
        break
    }
}
```

Now let's implement our didAccept function (Listing 4-18). Also, we will send a Hello! message to the client when the connection is established.

Listing 4-18. didAccept

```
private func didAccept(connection: NWConnection)
{
    let connection = ServerConnection(connection: connection)
    self.connections[connection.id] = connection
    connection.didStopCallback = { _ in
        self.connectionDidStop(connection: connection)
    }
    connection.start()
    connection.send(data: "Hello!! you are now a connection:
    \(connection.id)".data(using: .utf8)!)
    print("server did open connection \(connection.id)")
}
```

Now we will set up a callback function that will be called when the connection will be stopped (Listing 4-19).

In this function, we will just remove the connection from our list and display a message.

Listing 4-19. connectionDidStop

```
private func connectionDidStop(connection: ServerConnection)
{
    self.connections.removeValue(forKey: connection.id)
    print("server did close connection \(connection.id)")
}
```

The last function stop will be used to stop the server cleanly (Listing 4-20).

Listing 4-20. Stop

```
private func stop()
{
    self.listener?.stateUpdateHandler = nil
    self.listener?.newConnectionHandler = nil
    self.listener?.cancel()
    for connection in self.connections.values
    {
        connection.didStopCallback = nil
        connection.stop()
    }
    self.connections.removeAll()
}
```

With our Server and ServerConnection classes ready, we can implement our server functionality. Let's move to main.swift and import the Foundation framework (Listing 4-21).

Listing 4-21. Import

```
import Foundation
```

First, we are going to parse the arguments. The first argument will be the desired port number. After getting the port number from the arguments, we will start the server (Listing 4-22).

Again, we will place a version check at the top for Mac OS 14 onward.

Listing 4-22. Start Server

```swift
if #available(macOS 10.14, *)
{
    func initServer(port: UInt16)
    {
        let server = Server(port: port)
        do
        {
            try server.start()
        }
        catch let error
        {
            print("Failed to intialize server with error
            \(error.localizedDescription)")
        }
    }

    if let port = UInt16(CommandLine.arguments[1])
    {
      initServer(port: port)
    }
    else
    {
        print("Error invalid port")
    }

    RunLoop.current.run()
}
else
{
  let stderr = FileHandle.standardError
  let message = "Requires macOS 10.14 or newer"
```

```
stderr.write(message.data(using: .utf8)!)
exit(EXIT_FAILURE)
}
```

To test and debug the server from Xcode, you can pass command-line arguments by going to **Edit Scheme ➤ Run ➤ Arguments ➤ Arguments passed on launch** as shown in Figures 4-4 and 4-5.

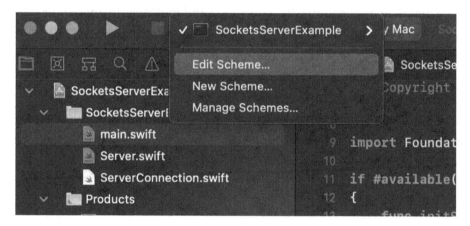

Figure 4-4. *Edit Scheme*

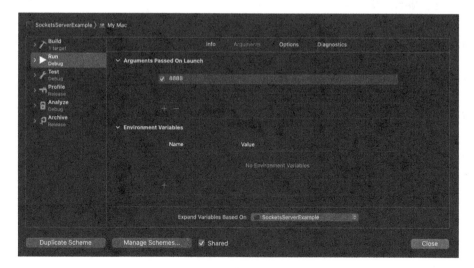

Figure 4-5. *Pass launch arguments*

With this, we are done with our server implementation and test setup. Now let's look into the client implementation.

Implementing Client Process

Create a new command-line application again, similar settings as the server, except this one is the SocketClientExample project.

This client application will allow us to send messages to any server. It will work with our server or with any other server that accepts a TCP connection.

Similar to what we did with ServerConnection, we are going to wrap the client NWConnection on its own object.

Let's create ClientConnection first. This is a connection wrapper which might seem similar to ServerConnection. Create the ClientConnection. swift file (Listings 4-23 and 4-24).

Listing 4-23. Imports

```
import Foundation
import Network
```

Listing 4-24. OS X version check

```
@available(macOS 10.14, *)
class ClientConnection
{

}
```

Let's look at the instance variables (Listing 4-25).

Listing 4-25. Instance variables

```
let connection: NWConnection
let maxPacketSize = 65536
let queue = DispatchQueue(label: "Client connection Q")
var didStopCallback: ((Error?) -> Void)? = nil
```

As can be seen, we are creating a DispatchQueue to manage the
asynchronous code. We have done this, so it doesn't block the main queue.
We want this so we can do other things in the main queue (like prompting
the user for a message to send, etc.).

Also, we declared the didStopCallback property; it will hold the closure
that will be executed when the connection stops.

Now we will look at the initializer (Listing 4-26) and start client
(Listing 4-27) functions.

Listing 4-26. Initializer

```
init(connection: NWConnection)
{
    self.connection = connection
}
```

Listing 4-27. Start function

```
func start()
{
    print("connection will start")
    connection.stateUpdateHandler = stateDidChange(to:)
    setupReceive()
    connection.start(queue: queue)
}
```

Now, we will implement stateDidChange (Listing 4-28) to track the
client connection state.

Listing 4-28. stateDidChange

```
private func stateDidChange(to state: NWConnection.State)
{
    switch state
    {
    case .waiting(let error):
        connectionDidFail(error: error)
    case .ready:
        print("Client connection ready")
    case .failed(let error):
        connectionDidFail(error: error)
    default:
        break
    }
}
```

Next, we will write a receive function (Listing 4-29) in which we will call the receive method of NWConnection with a completion block.

Listing 4-29. setupReceive

```
private func setupReceive()
{
    connection.receive(minimumIncompleteLength: 1,
    maximumLength: maxPacketSize) { (data, _, isComplete,
    error) in
        if let data = data, !data.isEmpty
        {
            let message = String(data: data, encoding: .utf8)
            print("connection did receive message: \(message ??
            "nil" )")
        }
```

```
        if isComplete
        {
            self.connectionDidEnd()
        }
        else if let error = error
        {
            self.connectionDidFail(error: error)
        }
        else
        {
            self.setupReceive()
        }
    }
}
```

Now, let's write a send method (Listing 4-30) to send data to the server.

Listing 4-30. Send

```
func send(data: Data)
{
    connection.send(content: data, completion:
    .contentProcessed( { error in
        if let error = error
        {
            self.connectionDidFail(error: error)
            return
        }
            print("connection did send data: \(data as
            NSData)")
    }))
}
```

Next is the implementation for connection did fail (Listing 4-31) and connection did end (Listing 4-32) methods.

Listing 4-31. connectionDidFail

```
private func connectionDidFail(error: Error)
{
    print("connection did fail with error: \(error)")
    self.stop(error: error)
}
```

Listing 4-32. connectionDidEnd

```
private func connectionDidEnd()
{
    print("connection did end")
    self.stop(error: nil)
}
```

At last, we will write the implementation for stop connection (Listings 4-33 and 4-34).

Listing 4-33. Stop

```
func stop()
{
    print("connection will stop")
    stop(error: nil)
}
```

Listing 4-34. Stop with error

```
private func stop(error: Error?)
{
    self.connection.stateUpdateHandler = nil
```

```swift
    self.connection.cancel()
    if let didStopCallback = self.didStopCallback
    {
        self.didStopCallback = nil
        didStopCallback(error)
    }
}
```

With this, we come to the end of ClientConnection.

Now we will create the Client.swift (Listing 4-35) file and will import the Network framework and implement a Mac OS version check (Listing 4-36).

Listing 4-35. Imports

```swift
import Foundation
import Network
```

Listing 4-36. OS X version check

```swift
@available(macOS 10.14, *)
class Client
{

}
```

Let's look at the instance variables (Listing 4-37).

Listing 4-37. Instance variables

```swift
var connection: ClientConnection?
private let host: NWEndpoint.Host
private var port: NWEndpoint.Port?
```

Now we will look at the initializer (Listing 4-38) and start client function (Listing 4-39).

Listing 4-38. Initializer

```
init(host: String, port: UInt16)
{
    self.host = NWEndpoint.Host(host)
    guard let endPoint = NWEndpoint.Port(rawValue: port) else
    {
        //End point port not found
        return
    }
    self.port = endPoint
    let connection = NWConnection(host: self.host, port: self.
    port!, using: .tcp)
    self.connection = ClientConnection(connection: connection)
}
```

Listing 4-39. Start client

```
func start()
{
    if self.port == nil
    {
        print("Client can not start")
    }
    print("Client started \(host) \(port!)")
    connection!.didStopCallback = didStopCallback(error:)
    connection!.start()
}
```

Next, we will implement a send method (Listing 4-40).

Listing 4-40. Send

```
func send(data: Data)
{
    connection?.send(data: data)
}
```

Last, we will implement stop methods (Listings 4-41 and 4-42).

Listing 4-41. Stop

```
func stop()
{
    connection?.stop()
}
```

Listing 4-42. didStopCallback

```
func didStopCallback(error: Error?)
{
    if error == nil
    {
        exit(EXIT_SUCCESS)
    }
    else
    {
        exit(EXIT_FAILURE)
    }
}
```

With our Client and ClientConnection classes ready, we have all we need to work on our main file and add the client code. We want to allow the user to enter a loop of sending messages and reading the response from the server, so we will add that to our main. First, import the Foundation framework (Listing 4-43).

Listing 4-43. Import

```
import Foundation
```

First, we are going to parse the arguments. The first argument will be the hostname which in our case is "localhost," and the second argument is the desired port number. After getting the port number from the arguments, we will start the client process.

Again, we will place a version check at the top for Mac OS 14 onward (Listing 4-44).

Listing 4-44. Start Client

```
if #available(macOS 10.14, *)
{
    let server = CommandLine.arguments[1]

    func initClient(server: String, port: UInt16)
    {
        let client = Client(host: server, port: port)
        client.start()
        while(true)
        {
            var command = readLine(strippingNewline: true)
            switch (command)
            {
                case "CRLF":
                    command = "\r\n"
                case "RETURN":
                    command = "\n"
                case "exit":
                    client.stop()
                default:
                    break
            }
        }
```

```
                client.connection?.send(data: (command?.data(using:
                .utf8))!)
            }
        }

        if let port = UInt16(CommandLine.arguments[2])
        {
            print("Starting as client, connecting to server:
            \(server) port: \(port)")
            initClient(server: server, port: port)
        }
        else
        {
            print("Error invalid port")
        }

        RunLoop.current.run()
}
else
{
    let stderr = FileHandle.standardError
    let message = "Requires macOS 10.14 or newer"
    stderr.write(message.data(using: .utf8)!)
    exit(EXIT_FAILURE)
}
```

We will provide some minimum set of commands as follows:

- **CRLF**: Send a Carriage Return Line Feed (\r\n) to the server.

- **Return**: Send a Line Feed (\n) to the server.

- **exit**: Close the connection.

To test and debug the client from Xcode, you can pass command-line arguments by going to **Edit Scheme ➤ Run ➤ Arguments ➤ Arguments passed on launch** as shown in Figures 4-4 and 4-6.

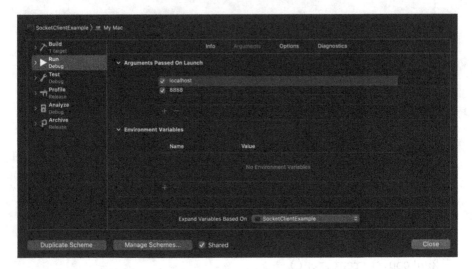

Figure 4-6. *Pass launch arguments*

With this, we are done with our client implementation and test setup.

Testing with Terminal

So far, we tested the setup with Xcode only. Now that we know that everything is working fine, it's time to run our app with a terminal app as a process.

To run the server first, open the terminal app. This app can be found in /Applications/Utilities.

Build the server project and drag the product, that is, "SocketsServerExample" app, on the terminal window and provide port 8080 for testing. You can provide any other free port as you like as shown in Figure 4-7.

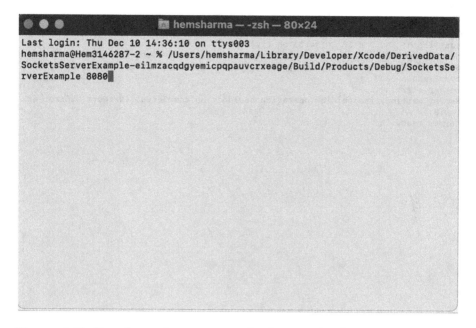

Figure 4-7. Pass launch arguments in the terminal

Press "Enter" and you will see the logs of the state transitioning of the server before starting as shown in Figure 4-8.

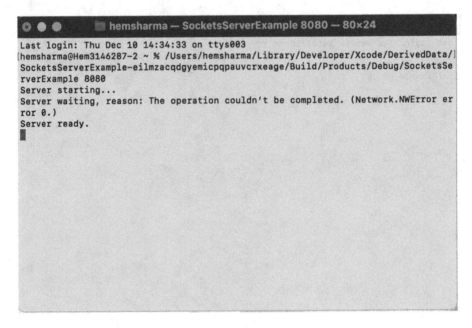

Figure 4-8. *Server state logs in the terminal*

Similarly, we will start the client process now by first building the client project and then dragging the product, that is, "SocketsClientExample" app, on the terminal window and provide port 8080 for testing. This port should match the port on which the server is running.

Here, we will pass two parameters (Figure 4-9). The first will be the hostname which in this case is localhost as we are running the server on the same machine as the client, and the second parameter will be the port name on which the server is running.

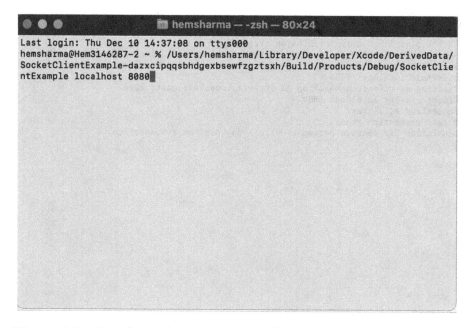

Figure 4-9. *Pass launch arguments in the terminal*

Now, when we press "Enter," we will see logs for the client sending data to the server and the server pinging back to the client as shown in Figures 4-10 and 4-11.

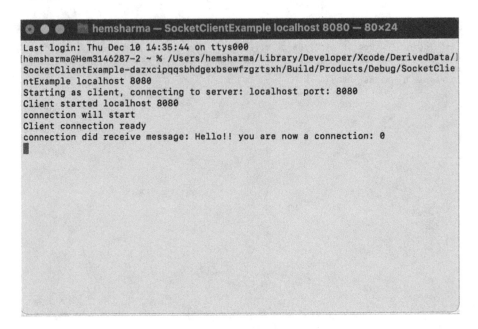

Figure 4-10. *Client got ping back from the server*

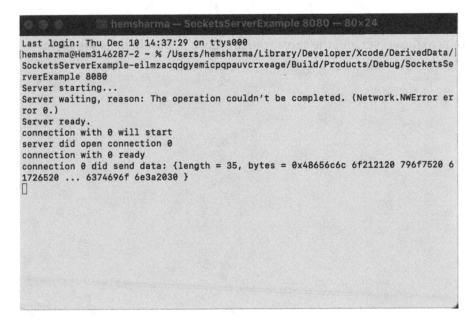

Figure 4-11. *Server received from the client*

Pros and Cons of IPC Using Sockets

Sockets are one-to-one. So, you will need multiple sockets if you want to send the same thing to multiple processes. With some other process like shared memory, you can have multiple readers and also multiple writers.

Also, Sockets are resource intensive. Each and every message goes through the OS, increasing the turnaround time of the process.

Sockets are intended for low volumes of data. For moving large volume of data during an IPC environment, a process like shared memory is more suitable.

Sockets are synchronized as long as you are not using UDP. With Sockets, synchronization is built in to the communication mechanism.

It's easy to convert a socket-based set of applications to one that uses network sockets. This can handle IPC between two processes on the same machine as well as on different machines.

Real-World Scenarios for IPC Using Sockets

If you are writing networking code that runs exclusively in macOS or if cross-platform portability is required, Sockets fulfill both categories. An application created to implement IPC to run exclusively in macOS can be easily extended to support cross-platform. In case you already have a backend code which you want to reuse in your application, this technique can be used effectively.

What's Next?

In this chapter, we discussed all about IPC using Sockets. Next, we will explore IPC using Apple Events. Stay tuned!

CHAPTER 5

IPC Through Apple Events

Apple Events are the only IPC mechanism which is universally supported by GUI applications on macOS for remote control. Operations like opening an application or telling an application to open a file or to quit and so on can be done using these.

Apple events provide a data transport and event dispatching mechanism that can be used for IPC between applications on the same computer or between applications on different computers connected to a network.

Apple events are generally used to request services and information from other applications or to provide services and information in response to such requests.

All macOS applications with GUI are able to respond to certain Apple events (also known as required events) sent by the OS itself. These include the open application, reopen, open documents, print documents, and quit events.

Some Apple Event Manager functions are thread safe. For others, you should call them only on the main thread.

In the Open Scripting Architecture (OSA), an Apple event is the basic message for IPC. In the OSA, Apple events are exchanged to establish communication between components.

© Hem Dutt 2021
H. Dutt, *Interprocess Communication with macOS*,
https://doi.org/10.1007/978-1-4842-7045-5_5

The Cocoa framework provides automatic handling for some Apple events that all applications can receive irrespective of whether the application is scriptable or not.

Apple events are processed as follows:

1. For the expected Apple event, an application registers callback routines (Apple event handler) with the Apple Event Manager.

2. When an application receives an Apple event, it dispatches the event to the appropriate handler using the Apple Event Manager.

AppleScript is a scripting language built on top of Apple Events which can be used using Scripting Bridge in a Mac application. We can use AppleScripts to perform IPC using Apple events.

Open Scripting Architecture (OSA)

The Open Scripting Architecture (OSA) provides an extensible and standard mechanism for IPC in macOS. Communication in the OSA is based on the exchange of Apple events.

In macOS, the OSA supports

1. The ability to create scriptable applications

2. The ability to create custom scripts to combine operations from multiple scriptable applications

3. The ability to implement IPC

Script Execution in the OSA

The OSA allows us to control multiple applications with scripts written in a variety of scripting languages. Each scripting language has a corresponding scripting component. The AppleScript component supports the AppleScript language, and this is the language which we will use in our implementation of IPC. When a scripting component executes a script, that script results in Apple events being sent to applications.

Although AppleScript is the most widely used language on macOS for scripting, developers can use the OSA to create scripting components for other scripting languages as well. Depending on the implementation, scripts written in these languages may or may not be able to communicate with scriptable applications.

Figure 5-1 shows the flow when the Script Editor application executes an AppleScript script that targets an application. The Script Editor invokes functions in the Open Scripting framework. The Open Scripting framework communicates through the AppleScript component, which further uses the Apple Event Manager to send required Apple events to the application. If a reply is requested, the application returns information in a reply Apple event.

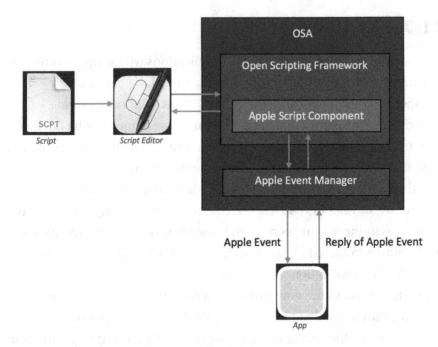

Figure 5-1. *Script execution in the OSA*

Scripting with AppleScript

AppleScript is a scripting language created by Apple. Using AppleScript, we can directly control scriptable Macintosh applications, as well as parts of macOS itself. We can create scripts to automate repetitive tasks, combine features from multiple scriptable applications, and create complex workflows.

A scriptable application is an application that can be controlled by a script. In the case of AppleScript, a scriptable application means being responsive to Apple events sent when a script command targets the application.

AppleScript does not provide a large number of commands, but it provides a robust framework into which you can plug many task-specific commands which are provided by scriptable applications and scriptable parts of macOS.

Script Editor

The **Script Editor** application is located in /Applications/Utilities. This application provides the ability to edit, compile, and execute scripts, display application scripting terminologies, and save scripts in a variety of formats, such as compiled scripts, applications, and plain text.

The Script Editor can display the result of executing an AppleScript script and can display logs of Apple events that are sent during the execution of a script. In the Script Editor Preferences, you can also choose to keep a history of recent results or event logs.

The Script Editor also has text formatting preferences for various types of script text, such as language keywords, comments, and so on. We can turn off or on the Script Assistant which can suggest and fill in scripting terms as we type. The Script Editor also provides a context menu to insert many types of boilerplate script statements, such as conditionals, comments, and error handlers.

The Script Editor application can display scriptable functions which are exposed by third-party applications in a dictionary window.

A dictionary is the part of a scriptable application for specifying the scripting terms it understands. We can choose File ➤ Open Dictionary in the Script Editor to display the dictionary of a scriptable application. Another way to open the dictionary is to drag an application icon to the Script Editor icon to display its dictionary.

To display a list that includes only the scriptable applications and scripting additions provided by macOS, choose Window ➤ Library. Double-click an item in the list to display its dictionary.

Figure 5-2 shows the list of scriptable applications available on a macOS system.

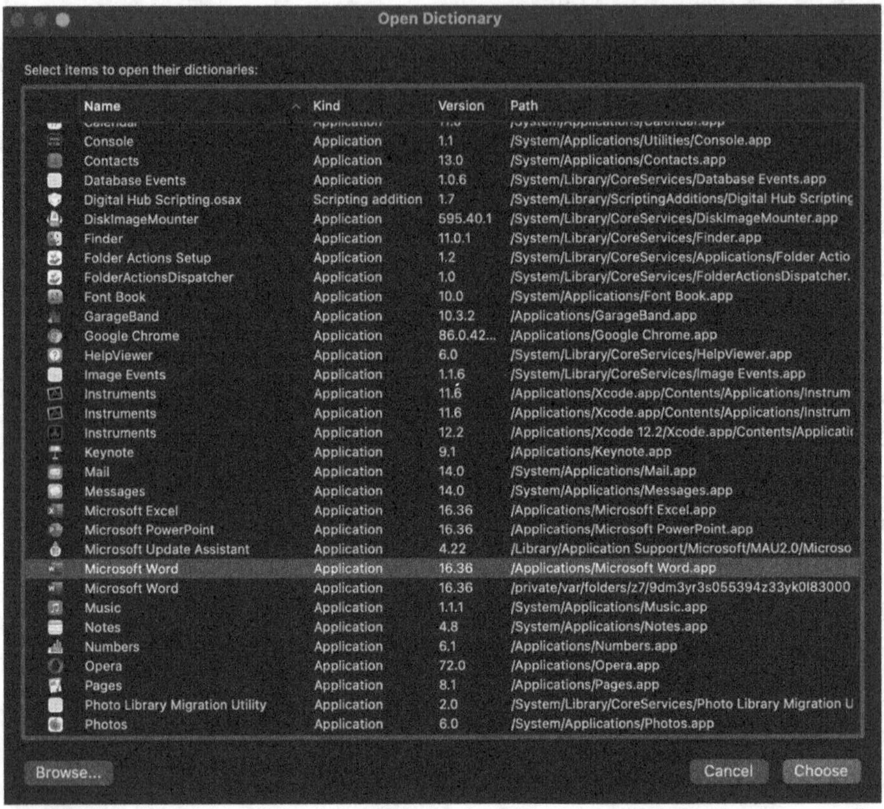

Open Dictionary

Select items to open their dictionaries:

Name	Kind	Version	Path
Calendar	Application	11.0	/System/Applications/Calendar.app
Console	Application	1.1	/System/Applications/Utilities/Console.app
Contacts	Application	13.0	/System/Applications/Contacts.app
Database Events	Application	1.0.6	/System/Library/CoreServices/Database Events.app
Digital Hub Scripting.osax	Scripting addition	1.7	/System/Library/ScriptingAdditions/Digital Hub Scripting
DiskImageMounter	Application	595.40.1	/System/Library/CoreServices/DiskImageMounter.app
Finder	Application	11.0.1	/System/Library/CoreServices/Finder.app
Folder Actions Setup	Application	1.2	/System/Library/CoreServices/Applications/Folder Actio
FolderActionsDispatcher	Application	1.0	/System/Library/CoreServices/FolderActionsDispatcher.
Font Book	Application	10.0	/System/Applications/Font Book.app
GarageBand	Application	10.3.2	/Applications/GarageBand.app
Google Chrome	Application	86.0.42...	/Applications/Google Chrome.app
HelpViewer	Application	6.0	/System/Library/CoreServices/HelpViewer.app
Image Events	Application	1.1.6	/System/Library/CoreServices/Image Events.app
Instruments	Application	11.6	/Applications/Xcode.app/Contents/Applications/Instrum
Instruments	Application	11.6	/Applications/Xcode.app/Contents/Applications/Instrum
Instruments	Application	12.2	/Applications/Xcode 12.2/Xcode.app/Contents/Applicati
Keynote	Application	9.1	/Applications/Keynote.app
Mail	Application	14.0	/System/Applications/Mail.app
Messages	Application	14.0	/System/Applications/Messages.app
Microsoft Excel	Application	16.36	/Applications/Microsoft Excel.app
Microsoft PowerPoint	Application	16.36	/Applications/Microsoft PowerPoint.app
Microsoft Update Assistant	Application	4.22	/Library/Application Support/Microsoft/MAU2.0/Microso
Microsoft Word	Application	16.36	/Applications/Microsoft Word.app
Microsoft Word	Application	16.36	/private/var/folders/z7/9dm3yr3s055394z33yk0l83000
Music	Application	1.1.1	/System/Applications/Music.app
Notes	Application	4.8	/System/Applications/Notes.app
Numbers	Application	6.1	/Applications/Numbers.app
Opera	Application	72.0	/Applications/Opera.app
Pages	Application	8.1	/Applications/Pages.app
Photo Library Migration Utility	Application	2.0	/System/Library/CoreServices/Photo Library Migration U
Photos	Application	6.0	/System/Applications/Photos.app

Browse...   Cancel   Choose

Figure 5-2. *Scriptable applications*

Figure 5-3 shows the dictionary for the Microsoft Word application in macOS.

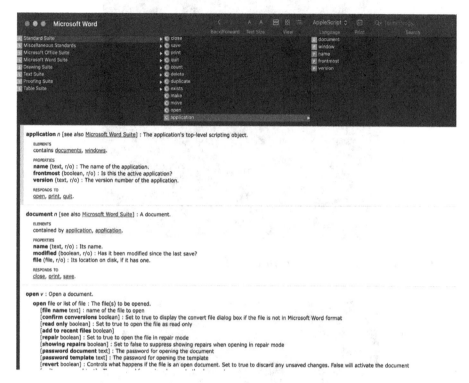

Figure 5-3. *Dictionary for MS Word*

Figure 5-4 shows various formats in which a file written in AppleScript can be saved. It is also possible to save the file as an application with .app extension along with other formats like script, txt file, and bundled script with .scptd extension.

If the script is saved as an application, there are options to show the start-up screen and let it run after the run handler as shown in Figure 5-5.

Figure 5-4. *AppleScript compile options*

Figure 5-5. *AppleScript compiled as an application bundle*

Scriptable Applications

A scriptable application is an application that goes beyond the basics of responding to Apple events sent by macOS. It makes its data and operations available to AppleScript scripts or to other applications. To make an application scriptable, the application must provide a terminology for scripters to use and the underlying Apple event code to support it. Cocoa applications can be made scriptable, and the Cocoa framework contains built-in support that minimizes the amount of code we have to write.

Scriptable applications need to describe the scripting terminology they support by supplying a scripting dictionary. A scripting dictionary specifies the commands and objects an application supports. It also specifies the information that is used by AppleScript or the application itself and possibly by other applications or scripts that want to take advantage of the application's scriptability.

For detailed information on designing the scripting terminology, refer to http://developer.apple.com/technotes/tn2002/tn2106.html.

There are three dictionary formats:

1. **sdef**: "sdef" is short for "scripting definition." This is an XML-based format. Cocoa applications can work natively with the sdef format. This is a superset of the following formats and supports new and improved features.

2. **script suite**: This is the original format used by Cocoa applications, and it is still supported for backward compatibility. An application can contain multiple script suites.

3. **aete**: This is the original dictionary format. The name comes from the Resource Manager resource type in which the information is stored ("aete").

A scriptable application typically responds to a set of common commands, such as get data, set data, save, and delete, as well as to other commands that support operations specific to the application.

Commands are represented in Apple events by constants defined in framework or application headers. To support a command, an application registers an event handler routine with the Apple Event Manager to handle Apple events it receives that specify that command.

The Apple Event Manager dispatches received events to the handlers registered for them.

For Cocoa applications, commands are registered automatically, so that developers rarely need to register Apple event handlers directly.

A recordable application is the application which sends Apple events to itself when a user performs actions with the application. If the user has turned on recording in the Script Editor application (with Script ➤ Record), actions that generate Apple events are recorded into an AppleScript script.

The Finder application in macOS is an example of a recordable application.

An application can create and send Apple events directly. This is usually done either by sending internal Apple events like in a recordable application, by obtaining services from a scriptable application, or by communicating directly with another application. The Open Scripting Architecture provides various mechanisms for creating and sending Apple events.

Applications can use Scripting Bridge to obtain services from scriptable applications. Scripting Bridge lets us work efficiently in a high-level language like Objective-C without troubling ourselves to handle the details of sending and receiving Apple events.

Interaction of Scriptable Application with Open Scripting Architecture (OSA)

The following flow of events explains how scriptable applications interact with the Open Scripting Architecture to expose their features to scripters:

1. The Apple Event Manager defines data structures that are used to construct Apple events.

2. The Open Scripting Architecture (OSA) provides a data transport and event dispatching mechanism for Apple events, built on top of lower-level protocols.

3. AppleScript defines a scripting language, described in the AppleScript Language Guide and implemented by the AppleScript component in macOS.

4. A scriptable application responds to additional common events, such as get data and set data, as well as to its own specific commands along with a small common set of Apple events sent by macOS, such as open application, quit, and open documents that all applications should respond to.

5. A scriptable application provides a scripting terminology (or dictionary) for the operations it supports. The sdef file format provides a mechanism for creating one terminology definition that can be converted for use in different environments.

6. Developers design their applications so that key operations can be invoked in response to received Apple events.

7. A scriptable application works with the Apple Event Manager to

    1. Register handlers for Apple events it can process

    2. Extract information from received Apple events and then perform requested operations or return requested data

    3. Construct Apple events for replies or other purposes

8. Scripters write AppleScript scripts that specify scriptable applications and the operations to perform.

9. When a script is executed, script statements that target applications are translated by the AppleScript component into Apple events that are sent to those applications.

10. Applications can also send Apple events directly to other applications.

11. An application responds to the Apple events it receives by performing operations, returning data, or both.

IPC Using AppleScript

As discussed in the previous sections of this chapter, Apple Events are the only IPC mechanism which is universally supported by GUI applications on macOS for remote control. Operations like opening an application or telling an application to open a file or to quit and so on can be done using these.

Let's go through some of the AppleScript examples implementing IPC on macOS.

Example 1

Tell the **Finder** application to launch the **Safari** application using AppleScript. Open the Script Editor and write code listed in Listing 5-1.

Listing 5-1. Launch Safari

```
-- Tell an application to launch Safari
tell application "Finder" to open application file (POSIX file
"/Applications/Safari.app")
```

Example 2

Tell the **Finder** application to close its front window using AppleScript. Open the Finder window. Now open the Script Editor and write code listed in Listing 5-2.

Listing 5-2. Close the Finder window

```
-- Tell Finder to close front window
tell application "Finder"
        set frontWin to name of front window
        close window frontWin
end tell
```

Example 3

Let us increase the complexity of the IPC process a little bit. Now we will try to update the font of a few words in a TextEdit document named "TestDocument.rtf".

Create a text document "TestDocument.rtf" and write some sample text in it as shown in Figure 5-6.

121

Figure 5-6. *TestDocument.rtf with sample text*

Now open the Script Editor and write code listed in Listing 5-3.

Listing 5-3. Change the font size and color of words in the document

```
-- Tell TextEdit to modify font and text color in specified
document
tell document "TestDocument" of application "TextEdit"
        set size of (words where it = "IPC") to 30
        set color of (words where it = "AppleEvent") to "red"
end tell
```

Results can be verified in Figure 5-7. The font and color of targeted words are updated successfully.

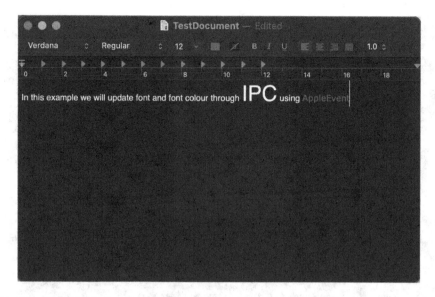

Figure 5-7. *TestDocument.rtf with updated text*

Example 4

Things are getting interesting now. Let's increase the heat a little more and try something more complex.

On macOS, information such as "creation date," "type," "size," and so on about a file or folder can be easily seen by cmd+click and selecting "Get Info" for the selected file in a panel as shown in the Figure 5-8.

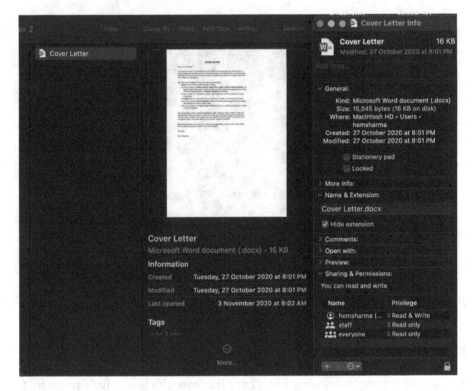

Figure 5-8. *Info panel for the Cover Letter document*

Let's explore how we can get the information programmatically using AppleScript by using APIs of the Finder application.

The script in Listing 5-4 will get the information as is shown by "Get Info" on Mac of the selected folder in Finder.

Listing 5-4. Get file information as shown in Get Info

```
tell application "Finder"
        -- Get information of 1st item from the list of all
            selected folders.
        -- To get info of all folders put the code in loop
        set selectedItem to (item 1 of (get selection))
```

```
    set informationList to {}
    copy ("FileName: " & displayed name of selectedItem) to
    end of informationList
    copy ("Type: " & kind of selectedItem) to end of
    informationList
    copy ("Size: " & size of selectedItem & " (" & physical
    size of selectedItem & ")") to end of informationList
    copy ("Where: " & (selectedItem as alias) as string) to
    end of informationList
    copy ("CreationDate: " & creation date of selectedItem)
    to end of informationList
    copy ("LastModified: " & modification date of
    selectedItem) to end of informationList
    --Full name of file or folder with extension
    copy ("FullName: " & name of selectedItem) to end of
    informationList
    copy ("IsLocked: " & locked of selectedItem) to end of
    informationList
end tell
set {delimiter, AppleScript's text item delimiters} to
{AppleScript's text item delimiters, return}
set infoAsString to informationList as string
```

Results can be verified in Figure 5-9 in the Script Editor console logs.

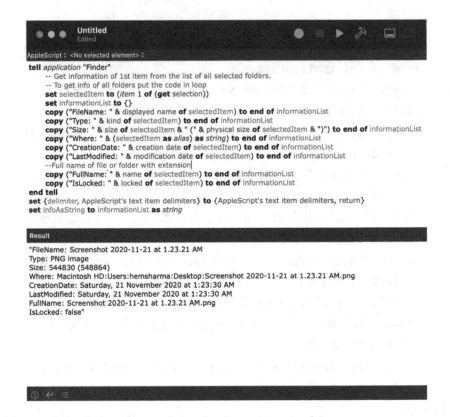

Figure 5-9. *Info recovered for the Cover Letter document*

All the examples discussed earlier from Listings 5-1 to 5-4 are implemented using AppleScript in the Script Editor application. Although these scripts can be bundled as a bundled script or a stand-alone application, it is often needed to invoke a script function from a native Cocoa app.

We will now look into the know-how of using AppleScripts within a Cocoa application.

AppleScript with Cocoa Application

There are a number of ways a Cocoa application can interact with AppleScript. One way is to launch AppleScript from a Cocoa application through a shell script or compile AppleScript as an app bundle and launch the app through a Cocoa app.

But the most efficient and effective way to invoke an AppleScript on the AppleScript handler in a Cocoa application is through the **NSAppleScript** class.

Let's look at the **Objective-C implementation** first and then we will dive into **Swift code** as well.

Invoking AppleScript Handler from Objective-C Code

First, create a new project and choose the "App" option for "macOS," as shown in Figure 5-10, with the Objective-C language, as shown in Figure 5-11.

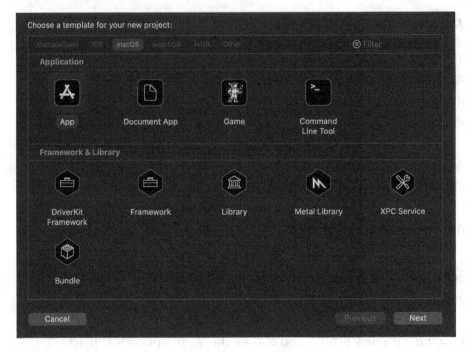

Figure 5-10. *Create an app for macOS*

We will name this project **ExampleAppleEvents**. In this project, we will write a generic code in Objective-C to launch the AppleScript.

To make our code modular, we will implement Objective-C code to invoke methods or handlers within the AppleScript, so that Objective-C code can selectively invoke AppleScript methods in an AppleScript and can also pass arguments from Objective-C code to AppleScript handlers.

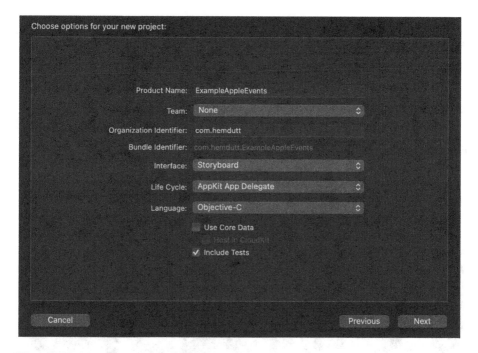

Figure 5-11. *Create an Objective-C project*

A non-sandboxed app has all the privileges of the user who is running that app and can access any resources that the user can access. If that app or the frameworks it is linked against contain security holes, an attacker can potentially exploit those loopholes to take control of that app. In doing so, the attacker gains the ability to do anything that the user can do.

A sandboxed app, on the other hand, has limited access to resources. Instead of having all the privileges of the user who is running that app, a sandboxed app must request entitlements for the resources it needs. By limiting access to resources, App Sandbox provides a last line of defense against the theft, corruption, or deletion of user data if an attacker successfully exploits security loopholes in your app or the frameworks it is linked against.

Because sandboxing limits interaction with files and folders and between apps in OS X, there are certain impacts on automation-related apps, such as scriptable apps, AppleScript apps, and Automator actions.

To be able to invoke AppleScripts from Cocoa code, we need to add a few entitlements in our app as shown in Figure 5-12.

As shown in Figure 5-12, we have to add an entitlement named "**Apple Events**" and set its Bool value to **YES**.

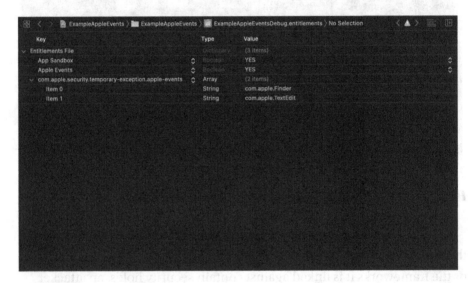

Figure 5-12. *Entitlements*

In case you are creating a **Sandboxed** application, you will have to add another entitlement named "**com.apple.security.temporary-exception. apple-events**" and add application identifiers for the application(s) you want to interact through Apple Events.

In this sample application, we will be interacting with **Finder** and **TextEdit** applications, and hence you can see two entries in entitlements for Finder and TextEdit, respectively.

This is not all; we are still not ready to implement an Apple Event–based IPC in our application.

Before writing any code, we need to add another entry in Info.plist as shown in Figure 5-13.

Add "Privacy – AppleEvents Sending Usage Description" and add a string message that you want to show to the user when a permission prompt appears on the screen for the user to allow the application to interact with other applications.

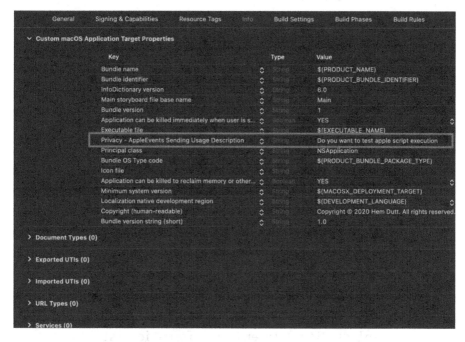

Figure 5-13. *App Info.plist*

Now we are ready to write some code. First, let's prepare our modular AppleScripts. In this sample, we are going to write two sample AppleScripts exposing their methods/handlers, and we will see how we can pass parameters from the Cocoa app to AppleScript.

In Listing 5-5, we will reuse AppleScript from Listing 5-4 but with a more modular approach by creating a method returning the value to the Cocoa app.

131

Listing 5-5. Get file information as shown in Get Info using AppleScript handlers

```
on displayInfo()
    tell application "Finder"
        -- Get information of 1st item from the list of all
           selected folders.
        -- To get info of all folders put the code in loop
        set selectedItem to (item 1 of (get selection))
        set informationList to {}
        copy ("FileName: " & displayed name of
        selectedItem) to end of informationList
        copy ("Type: " & kind of selectedItem) to end of
        informationList
        copy ("Size: " & size of selectedItem & " (" &
        physical size of selectedItem & ")") to end of
        informationList
        copy ("Where: " & (selectedItem as alias) as
        string) to end of informationList
        copy ("CreationDate: " & creation date of
        selectedItem) to end of informationList
        copy ("LastModified: " & modification date of
        selectedItem) to end of informationList
        --Full name of file or folder with extension
        copy ("FullName: " & name of selectedItem) to end
        of informationList
        copy ("IsLocked: " & locked of selectedItem) to end
        of informationList
    end tell
```

```
        set {delimiter, AppleScript's text item delimiters} to
        {AppleScript's text item delimiters, return}
        set infoAsString to informationList as string
        return infoAsString
end displayInfo
```

To see how a parameterized AppleScript method can be called from the macOS app, we will reuse AppleScript from Listing 5-3 but with a more modular approach by creating a method which can accept parameters as shown in Listing 5-6.

Listing 5-6. Change the font size and color of words in the document

```
on highlightWordInTextDocument(documentName, wordToHighlight)
    tell document documentName of application "TextEdit"
            set size of (words where it = wordToHighlight)
            to 30
            set color of (words where it = wordToHighlight)
            to "red"
    end tell
end highlightWordInTextDocument
```

Save both these scripts with .scpt extension and name "**Sample_Script1.scpt**" and "**Sample_Script2.scpt**", respectively.

Add these to your application bundle by dragging the scripts in the Xcode project.

Now we are ready to dive into Objective-C code to invoke methods written in "**Sample_Script1.scpt**" and "**Sample_Script2.scpt**", respectively, and to perform IPC through Apple Events from a macOS application.

Add the Carbon framework to the project.

In the ViewController class in the **ExampleAppleEvents** project, write functions to execute the AppleScripts.

We need to import the Carbon framework (Listing 5-7) in ViewController because we need constant values for the script suite, transaction id, and subroutine events.

Listing 5-7. Imports

```
#import <Carbon/Carbon.h>
```

Now let's create a UI to invoke the AppleScripts and show results of the function execution. Go to the main storyboard and add a TextView and Button titled "Run Apple Scripts" on the View Controller Scene as shown in Figure 5-14.

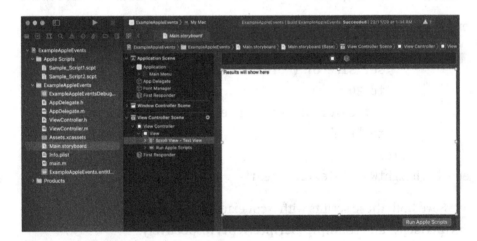

Figure 5-14. *Add a TextView and Button on the UI*

In the ViewController.h class, create an IBOutlet for TextView and also declare a button action (Listing 5-8).

Listing 5-8. Create an IBOutlet for TextView and declare a button action

```
@interface ViewController : NSViewController{
    IBOutlet NSTextView* textView;
}

-(IBAction)runAppleScripts:(id)sender;

@end
```

Right-click the TextView in Main.storyboard and link its reference outlet with the "textView" property of the ViewController class.

Again, right-click the button in Main.storyboard and link its action with the function "runAppleScripts" in the ViewController class.

Next, we will write a generic function in Objective-C which will be able to invoke AppleScript at a given path or a particular method in the AppleScript at a given path.

This function implementation would empower the application to pass input parameters to an AppleScript method and get a return value from it (Listing 5-9).

Listing 5-9. Generic Objective-C code to invoke AppleScript methods

```
- (NSString *) executeScriptWithPath:(NSString*)path
  function:(NSString*)functionName andArguments:(NSArray*)
  scriptArgumentArray
{

    NSAppleScript* appleScript;
    NSAppleEventDescriptor* thisApplication;
    NSAppleEventDescriptor* containerEvent;
    NSURL* pathURL = [NSURL fileURLWithPath:path];
```

```
NSDictionary * appleScriptCreationError = nil;
appleScript = [[NSAppleScript alloc] initWithContentsOf
URL:pathURL error:&appleScriptCreationError];

if (appleScriptCreationError)
{
    NSLog(@"%@", [NSString stringWithFormat:@"Could not
    instantiate applescript %@",appleScriptCreationError]);
    return [NSString stringWithFormat:@"Could not
    instantiate applescript %@",appleScriptCreationError];
}
else
{
    if (functionName && [functionName length])
    {
        //If we have a functionName (and/or arguments), we
            will build an NSAppleEvent to execute the script.

        //Get a descriptor for ourself
        int pid = [[NSProcessInfo processInfo]
        processIdentifier];
        thisApplication = [NSAppleEventDescriptor
        descriptorWithDescriptorType:typeKernelProcessID
                                    bytes:&pid
                                    length:sizeof(pid)];

        //Create the container event
        AEEventClass eventClass = kASAppleScriptSuite;
        AEEventID eventId = kASSubroutineEvent;
```

```objc
containerEvent = [NSAppleEventDescriptor appleEvent
                WithEventClass:eventClass
                eventID:eventId
            targetDescriptor:thisApplication
                returnID:kAutoGenerateReturnID
            transactionID:kAnyTransactionID];

//Set the target function
[containerEvent setParamDescriptor:[NSAppleEvent
Descriptor descriptorWithString:functionName]
        forKeyword:keyASSubroutineName];

//Pass arguments - arguments is expecting an
  NSArray with only NSString objects
if ([scriptArgumentArray count])
{
    NSAppleEventDescriptor  *arguments = [[NSApple
    EventDescriptor alloc] initListDescriptor];
    NSString *object;

    for (object in scriptArgumentArray)
    {
        [arguments insertDescriptor:[NSAppleEventDe
        scriptor descriptorWithString:object]
                    atIndex:([arguments
                    numberOfItems] + 1)]; //This +1
                    seems wrong... but it's not
    }

    [containerEvent setParamDescriptor:arguments
    forKeyword:keyDirectObject];
}
```

```
//Execute the event
NSDictionary * executionError = nil;
NSAppleEventDescriptor * result = [appleScript
executeAppleEvent:containerEvent error:&execution
Error];
if (executionError != nil)
{
    NSLog(@"%@", [NSString stringWithFormat:
    @"error while executing script. Error %@",
    executionError]);
    return [NSString stringWithFormat:@"error while
    executing script. Error %@",executionError];

}
else
{
    NSLog(@"Script execution has succeed.
    Result(%@)",result);
    return [NSString stringWithFormat:@"%@",
    result];
}
}
else
{
    NSDictionary * executionError = nil;
    NSAppleEventDescriptor * result = [appleScript exec
uteAndReturnError:&executionError];

    if (executionError != nil)
    {
        NSLog(@"%@", [NSString stringWithFormat:@"
        error while executing script. Error %@",
        executionError]);
```

```
            return [NSString stringWithFormat:@"error while
            executing script. Error %@",executionError];
        }
        else
        {

            NSLog(@"Script execution has succeed.
            Result(%@)",result);
            return [NSString stringWithFormat:@"%@",
            result];
        }
    }
  }
}
```

Now, in the ViewController class, add a button action to invoke AppleScript methods from the application (Listing 5-10).

Listing 5-10. Invoke AppleScript methods

```
-(IBAction) runAppleScripts:(id)sender
{
    NSString* resultOfScript1 = [self executeScriptWithPath:
    [[NSBundle mainBundle] pathForResource:@"Sample_Script1"
    ofType:@"scpt"] function:@"displayInfo" andArguments:nil];
     NSLog(@"%@", resultOfScript1);

    //Run script 2 to highlight certain word in a text document
    [self executeScriptWithPath:[[NSBundle mainBundle]
    pathForResource:@"Sample_Script2" ofType:@"scpt"] function:
    @"highlightWordInTextDocument" andArguments:[NSArray
    arrayWithObjects:@"TestDocument",@"AppleEvent", nil]];
}
```

Invoking AppleScript Handler from Swift Code

Now let's look into Swift implementation of the code described above. Again create a new project as shown in Figure 5-10 and name it **ExampleAppleEvents-Swift**. Instead of selecting Objective-C language as shown in Figure 5-11, choose Swift. The tasks shown in Figure 5-12 till 5-14 will still be valid for the Swift project as well.

In ViewController class create a IBOutlet for TextView and also define a button action (Listing 5-11).

Listing 5-11. Create IBoutlet and Button action function

```
class ViewController: NSViewController {

    @IBOutlet var textView : NSTextView!

    @IBAction func executeBothAppleScripts(sender : Any){
        let resultOfScript1 = self.executeScriptWith(pathURL:
        Bundle.main.url(forResource: "Sample_Script1",
        withExtension: "scpt")!, functionName: "displayInfo",
        argumentsArray: nil)
        textView.string = resultOfScript1;
    }
}
```

Next we will write a generic function in Swift which will be able to invoke AppleScript at a given path or a particular method in the AppleScript at a given path (Listing 5-12), similar to Listing 5-9.

Listing 5-12. Generic Swift code to invoke Apple script methods

```
private func executeScriptWith(pathURL : URL, functionName :
String?, argumentsArray : Array<String>?) -> String{

        var appleScriptCreationError : NSDictionary?
```

```
let appleScript = NSAppleScript.init(contentsOf:
pathURL, error: &appleScriptCreationError)
guard appleScriptCreationError == nil else {
    return "\(String(describing: appleScriptCreationError))"
}

if let function = functionName, function.count > 0{
    var pid = ProcessInfo.processInfo.processIdentifier
    let thisApplication = NSAppleEventDescriptor.
    init(descriptorType: typeKernelProcessID, bytes:
    &pid, length: MemoryLayout.size(ofValue: pid))
    let eventClass = AEEventClass(kASAppleScriptSuite)
    let eventId = AEEventID(kASSubroutineEvent)
    let containerEvent = NSAppleEventDescriptor.
    appleEvent(withEventClass: eventClass, eventID:
    eventId , targetDescriptor: thisApplication,
    returnID: AEReturnID(kAutoGenerateReturnID),
    transactionID: AETransactionID(kAnyTransactionID))
    let targetFunction = NSAppleEventDescriptor.
    init(string: function)
    containerEvent.setParam(targetFunction, forKeyword:
    AEKeyword(keyASSubroutineName))

    if let arguments = argumentsArray,
    arguments.count > 0{
        let eventArguments = NSAppleEventDescriptor.
        init(listDescriptor: ())
        for object in arguments{
            eventArguments.insert(NSAppleEventDescriptor.
            init(string: object), at: eventArguments.
            numberOfItems + 1)
        }
```

```swift
            containerEvent.setParam(eventArguments,
            forKeyword: keyDirectObject)
        }

        var appleScriptExecutionError : NSDictionary?
        let result = appleScript?.executeAppleEvent
        (containerEvent, error: &appleScriptExecutionError)
        if appleScriptExecutionError == nil {
            //Success
            return "\(String(describing: result))"
        }
        else{
            //Failure
            return "\(String(describing:
            appleScriptExecutionError))"
        }
    }
    else{
        var appleScriptExecutionError : NSDictionary?
        let result = appleScript?.executeAndReturnError
        (&appleScriptExecutionError)
        if appleScriptExecutionError == nil {
            //Success
            return "\(String(describing: result))"
        }
        else{
            //Failure
            return "\(String(describing:
            appleScriptExecutionError))"
        }
    }
}
```

Run the application and click the button "**Run Apple Scripts**." Before this make sure that you have anitem selected in Finder for which you want to extract information. You will see the results on the TextView in the application window.

Scripting Bridge

Scripting Bridge is a technology which makes it easy for a program written in Objective-C to communicate with scriptable applications.

Many applications on OS X are scriptable. A scriptable application must define an interface for responding to commands. This interface and its implementation must conform to an object model prescribed by the Open Scripting Architecture (OSA) that specifies the classes of scripting objects, the accessible properties of those objects, the inheritance and containment relationships of scripting objects, and the commands that the scriptable application responds to.

The OSA packages commands to scriptable applications as Apple events and uses the Apple Event Manager to dispatch those events and receive data in return.

AppleScript scripts have long been the principal way to communicate with scriptable applications. But an application can also send commands to a scriptable application and receive responses back to it.

The traditional way of doing this requires you to use the data structures and functions of the OSA framework to create and send Apple events, but this can be a very complex task.

Typical Cocoa applications, if not using Scripting Bridge, rely on including an AppleScript script in the application bundle and use Cocoa's NSAppleScript class to execute the script as we have discussed in sections before.

Another way a Cocoa app interacts with scriptable applications is by using the NSAppleEventDescriptor class to create Apple events which they then send with Apple Event Manager routines.

However, both of these approaches are not straightforward for Cocoa developers not interested in AppleScripts.

The Scripting Bridge framework makes it possible to send and receive Apple events using Objective-C messages instead of AppleScript commands or Apple event descriptors.

For Cocoa programmers, Scripting Bridge provides a very simple model for controlling scriptable applications. It allows Cocoa programs to send and receive Apple events without requiring you to have detailed knowledge of the target application's Apple event model.

Scripting Bridge integrates well with existing Objective-C code and works with standard Cocoa designs, such as key-value coding, target-action, and declared properties.

Other advantages of Scripting Bridge are

1. It gives your application access to any scriptable feature of any available scriptable application.

2. It uses native Cocoa data types like NSString, NSArray, NSURL, and so on so that you'll never have to deal with less familiar Carbon types.

3. It manages Apple event data structures automatically, using standard Cocoa memory management to allocate and free Apple events.

4. It requires much less code than needed to use NSAppleEventDescriptor and direct Apple Event Manager calls.

5. It checks for compile time syntax errors, unlike NSAppleScript.

6. It runs more than twice as fast as a precompiled NSAppleScript and up to 100 times as fast as an uncompiled NSAppleScript.

7. As Scripting Bridge dynamically populates an application's namespace with Objective-C objects representing the items defined by an application's scripting definition, it enables other scripting languages bridged to Objective-C, namely, RubyCocoa and PyObjC, to communicate with and control scriptable applications.

How Scripting Bridge Works?

When you request an instance of a scriptable application from Scripting Bridge, it first locates the bundle of the application by a bundle identifier, URL, or process identifier.

It then gets from the bundle the scripting definition of the application contained in its sdef file and parses it. From the items in the scripting definition—classes, properties, elements, commands, and so on—it dynamically declares and implements Objective-C classes corresponding to the scripting classes of the application. The dynamically generated classes inherit from one of the classes defined by the Scripting Bridge framework, **SBObject**.

When you ask an object for the objects it contains, Scripting Bridge instantiates those objects from the appropriate scripting classes and returns them. If you request the objects contained by one of those objects, Scripting Bridge instantiates new scripting objects from the appropriate class and returns those. This process continues until you reach a leaf node of the graph, which is typically a property containing actual data.

At the root of the object graph is the instance of a dynamically generated subclass of **SBApplication** that represents the application object. For other scripting objects in the object graph, Scripting Bridge uses an instance of a dynamically generated SBObject subclass. Elements, which specify "to-many" relationships with other scripting objects, are implemented as methods that return instances of **SBElementArray**.

Scripting Bridge implements commands and properties as methods of the SBApplication subclass or of one of the application's scripting classes. It implements the properties of a class as Objective-C declared properties, which results in the synthesis of accessor methods for those properties.

Many of these accessor methods return, and sometimes set, objects of an appropriate Foundation or Application Kit type, such as NSString, NSURL, NSColor, and NSNumber. These properties represent the concrete data of a scriptable application.

For commands, Scripting Bridge evaluates the direct parameter to determine the class to assign the method implementation to. If it's a specific scripting class, the command becomes a method of that class, but if it's of a generic class, it becomes a method of the SBApplication subclass.

Scripting objects in Scripting Bridge derived from SBObject are essentially object specifiers. That is, they are references to objects in the scriptable application. To get or set concrete data in the application, the scripting object must be evaluated, which results in Scripting Bridge sending an Apple event to the application.

Working with Scripting Bridge

Scripting Bridge code is like any other Objective-C code barring a few differences due to the OSA architecture on which the dispatch and handling of Apple events is based. In this chapter, we will discuss how to use Scripting Bridge in Objective-C projects.

Code Preparation

Before we begin writing any Scripting Bridge code for our project, there are a few steps we should complete:

1. Generate header files for all scriptable applications that our code intends to send messages.

2. Add these files to the project.

3. In the header or implementation files, add #import statements for the generated header files.

4. Add the Scripting Bridge framework to the project.

A header file that is generated for a scriptable application serves as a reference documentation for the scripting classes of that application. It includes information about the inheritance relationships between classes and the containment relationships between their objects. It also shows how commands, properties, and elements are declared. Taking the Safari application as an example, the header file shows the definition of the application class (SafariApplication), the application's scripting classes (such as SafariDocument and SafariWindow), and so on. A header file also includes comments extracted from the scripting definition.

To create the header file for a scriptable application, we need to run two command-line tools, sdef and sdp, together, with the output from one piped to the other. The recommended syntax is

```
sdef /path/to/application.app | sdp -fh --basename
applicationName
```

The sdef utility gets the scripting definition from the designated application. If that application does not contain an sdef file, but does instead contain scripting information in an older format, it translates that information into the sdef format first. The sdp tool generates an Objective-C header file for the designated scriptable application. Hence, for Safari, we will run the command in Listing 5-13 to produce a header file named Safari.h.

Listing 5-13. Creating a header for the Safari app

```
sdef /Applications/Safari.app | sdp -fh --basename Safari
```

Add the generated file to the Xcode project by dragging the file and dropping on the Xcode project or by choosing Add to Project from the Project menu and specifying the file in the ensuing dialog. In any source or header file in your project that references Scripting Bridge objects, insert the appropriate #import statements, such as the one in Listing 5-14.

Listing 5-14. Importing a header for the Safari app

```
#import "Safari.h"
```

Add the Scripting Bridge framework to the project using the Project ➤ Add to Project menu command.

Creating Application Object and Controlling Scriptable Application

Before we can send messages to a scriptable application, we need to create an object that represents the application. The Scripting Bridge framework declares three class factory methods for creating instances of scriptable applications.

For creating an instance of a scriptable application, we will use the function applicationWithBundleIdentifier:. The method can locate an application on a system even if the user has renamed the application, and it doesn't require us to know the application's location on disk. The line of code in Listing 5-15 creates an instance of the Safari application.

Listing 5-15. Creating an object for the Safari app

```
SafariApplication* safariApp = [SBApplication applicationWith
BundleIdentifier:@"com.apple.safari"];
```

An application's bundle identifier can be found by looking for the value of the CFBundleIdentifier property in the Info.plist file stored in the application bundle.

To control a scriptable application, as any other class, send to the instance of the application's object a message based on a method declared by the object's class. These methods correspond to commands in the application's scripting definition. The action method listed in Listing 5-16 logs the currently open window names in the Safari application.

Listing 5-16. Log name of windows currently opened in the Safari app

```
NSLog(@"%@",safariApp.version);
SBElementArray *documentItems = [safariApp windows];
for (SafariWindow *item in documentItems)
{
    NSLog(@"%@",item.name);
}
```

With this, we come to an end of this chapter and are done with IPC using Apple Events. For getting more information on AppleScripts, please refer to https://developer.apple.com/library/archive/documentation/AppleScript/Conceptual/AppleScriptLangGuide/introduction/ASLR_intro.html.

Pros and Cons of IPC Using Apple Events

AppleScript is a scripting language used to automate the actions of the Macintosh Operating System and many of its applications.

AppleScript can perform a task as simple as copying a file or parsing an XML file or as complex as building a real estate catalog.

AppleScript is the most powerful, easy-to-use, automation tool available on and supported by macOS.

149

AppleScript is very much like the English language. AppleScript's greatest advantage is that it uses grammar that closely resembles the commands you'd give in natural language.

AppleScript doesn't bother you with semicolons, curly brackets, and all the other distractions of more advanced computer languages. On top of that, AppleScript is not case-sensitive and that you will appreciate only if you've ever had to search through a pile of code just to find a miscapitalized command name.

It works seamlessly with the third-party programs that you generally use for day-to-day work, and you can easily automate a lot of your tasks with these applications using AppleScript.

Virtually every big-name Mac program supports AppleScript commands: Microsoft Word, Adobe Photoshop, FileMaker Pro, and so on. Lots of free programs support AppleScript too like Address Book, TextEdit, Mail, iPhoto, and many more.

It works seamlessly with other computer languages and Cocoa applications. AppleScript got bridges to virtually every other programming language on macOS.

Despite all its advantages, however, AppleScript has its own trade-offs to make it more like English.

Some programs don't support AppleScript at all as not all applications need to be scriptable. Programs that show up in this category are usually old, free, and/or made by a company that doesn't make macOS-only applications.

In exchange for all the power AppleScript grants you, it's slower than most other languages and has an unusually high overhead for running commands. If speed is of utmost importance to you, you might want to look somewhere else for a language that better suits your needs.

It only works with macOS. If you're only going to write scripts for your computer, this isn't a big deal. But if you need to exchange scripts with Windows or Linux users, you'll need to find a cross-platform language.

Real-World Scenarios for IPC Using Apple Events

Apple Event–based IPC is generally used to automate a repetitive task which involves a third-party scriptable app in the workflow.

For example, if there is a business use case where there is a folder in which multiple Excel files gets dumped every day, having some business data like daily sales figures or various other financial data which you want to sort based on certain criteria and manually opening each file and performing formulas in them is tedious. In this case, you can use Apple Events to use exposed scriptable features of the Excel app to perform the desired tasks automatically.

Another example is of the Pixelmator app. As the introductory documentation of the Pixelmator app says, "Pixelmator Pro includes extensive and full-featured support for AppleScript.

There are many different ways you can use AppleScript to speed up and enhance your image editing workflows. For example, you can use it to automate repetitive tasks, such as changing the color of the background in, say, 100 images to a specific shade of blue. You can also create workflows that involve multiple applications—for example, if you need to take a set of texts from a Numbers spreadsheet and use them to label a series of images. You can even use AppleScript to extend the functionality of Pixelmator Pro itself, for example by writing a script that creates a 3D text effect using the built-in tools in the app."

Another example of using Apple events to automate an otherwise tedious and nonproductive task is when you sync and share many calendars in iCal, and you often end up with a lot of duplicates.

A simple AppleScript can help you remove those duplicates automatically.

Another real-world example could be to automate the deletion of Safari icons, cache, and plist files. Getting rid of these extraneous files can boost Safari's performance.

There are various other examples which involve IPC using Apple Events to make it easy and fast by automating certain tasks which otherwise would need considerable human effort and time.

What's Next?

We have made it so far covering various IPC techniques together. All these techniques looked really scary in the beginning, but I hope after following the chapters and code, it was fun.

Till now, we have discussed low-level IPC techniques which work quite well with the Cocoa project but still are not at the abstraction level of Cocoa applications. In the next chapters, we will discuss high-level IPC techniques. So, stay tuned and enjoy coding!

CHAPTER 6

IPC Through Distributed Notifications

The Foundation framework provides a programming architecture
for passing around information about the occurrence of events. This
architecture (Figure 6-1) deals with notifications and the notification
center.

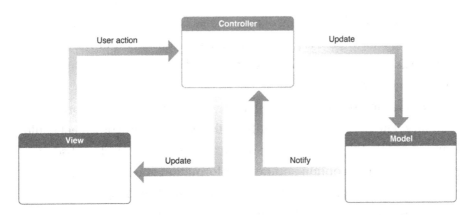

Figure 6-1. *MVC design pattern diagram from developer.apple.com*

© Hem Dutt 2021
H. Dutt, *Interprocess Communication with macOS*,
https://doi.org/10.1007/978-1-4842-7045-5_6

Notifications

A notification encapsulates information about an event, for example, a background sync operation with a server gets completed or a network connection is closing. Objects that need to know about an event are also known as observers, for example, a document that needs to know when its window is about to be closed registers with the notification center that it wants to be notified when that event happens.

When the event actually happens, a notification is posted to the notification center, which immediately broadcasts this notification to all registered objects. Optionally, a notification is queued in a notification queue, which posts notifications to a notification center after it delays specified notifications and coalesces notifications that are similar according to some criteria you specify.

The standard way to pass information between objects is message passing, that is, one object invokes the method of another object. However, message passing basically requires that the object sending the message know who the receiver is and what messages it responds to.

At times, this tight coupling of two objects is undesirable. For such cases, a broadcast model is provided by the Foundation framework. An object posts a notification, which is dispatched to the observers through a NotificationCenter.

A Notification object contains a name, an object, and an optional dictionary. The name is a tag identifying the notification. The object could be any object that the poster of the notification wants to send to observers. The dictionary may contain additional information about the event.

Any object may post a notification. Other objects can register themselves with the notification center as observers to receive notifications when they are posted. The notification center handles broadcasting of notifications to the registered observers.

The object posting the notification, the object included in the notification, and the observer of the notification may all be different objects or the same object. Objects that post notifications need not know anything about the observers. On the other hand, observers need to know at least the notification name and structure of the dictionary if provided.

Using the notification system is similar to using the delegation pattern but has the following differences:

- Any number of objects can receive the notification, not just the delegate object.

- An object can receive any message by registering for the event name, not just the predefined delegate methods.

- The object posting the notification does not need to know the observer exists.

Notification Center

The notification center manages the sending and receiving of notifications. It notifies all observers of notifications. The notification information is encapsulated in NSNotification objects.

Client objects register themselves with the notification center as observers of specific notifications. When an event occurs, an object posts an appropriate notification to the notification center.

The notification center sends a message to each registered observer, passing the notification as the sole argument. It is possible that the posting object and the observing object are the same.

Cocoa includes two types of notification centers.

NotificationCenter

This class manages notifications within a single process.

Each process has a default notification center that can be accessed with the NotificationCenter's class var "default" in Swift and +defaultCenter class method in Objective-C. This notification center handles notifications within a single process.

A notification center delivers notifications to observers synchronously.

This means that when posting a notification, the control does not return to the poster until all observers have received and processed the notification. To send notifications asynchronously, we can use a notification queue.

In a multithreaded environment, notifications are always delivered in the thread in which the notification was posted, which may not be the same thread in which an observer registered itself.

DistributedNotificationCenter

This class manages notifications across multiple processes on a single computer.

Each process has a default distributed notification center that you access with the DistributedNotificationCenter's class var "default" in Swift and +defaultCenter class method in Objective-C. This distributed notification center handles notifications that can be sent between different processes on a single machine.

Posting a distributed notification is an expensive operation. The notification gets dispatched to a system-wide server and then gets broadcasted to all the processes that have objects which registered for distributed notifications. This adds an unbounded latency between posting the notification and the notification's arrival in another process. It is possible that, if too many notifications are being posted and the server's queue fills up, notifications can be dropped.

Distributed notifications are delivered through a process's run loop. A process must be running a run loop in one of the "common" modes, such as NSDefaultRunLoopMode, to receive a distributed notification. If the receiving process is running in a multithreaded environment, do not depend on the notification arriving on the main thread. The notification usually gets delivered to the main thread's run loop, but other threads could also receive the notification.

Though a regular notification center allows any object to be observed, a distributed notification center is restricted to observing a string object, because the posting object and the observer may be in different processes, and hence notifications cannot contain pointers to arbitrary objects. Hence, a distributed notification center requires notifications to use a string as the notification object. Notification matching is done based on this string rather than an object pointer.

In this chapter, we will focus only on the distributed notifications, and these are the ones which provide IPC capabilities. Our discussion on local notifications will be very limited in this chapter.

Registering for a Notification

You can register for notifications from within your own application, that is, for a local notification, or from other applications, that is, distributed notification. You also need to unregister for a notification, which must be done when your observer object gets deallocated.

Registering for Local Notifications

To register an object to receive a notification, we should invoke the notification center method addObserver:selector:name:object:, specifying the observer, the message the notification center should send to the observer, the name of the notification it wants to receive, and about which object.

No need to specify both the name and the object. If we specify only the object, the observer will receive all notifications containing that object. If we specify a notification name, the observer will receive that notification every time it's posted, regardless of the object associated with it.

It is possible for an observer to register to receive more than one message for the same notification. In such a case, the observer will receive all messages it is registered to receive for the notification, but the order in which it receives them cannot be determined.

If we later decide that an observer no longer needs to receive notifications, we can remove the observer from the notification center's list of observers with the methods removeObserver: or removeObserver:name:object:.

Normally, we register objects with the process's default notification center. We can obtain the default object using the defaultCenter class method.

As an example of using the notification center to receive notifications, suppose we want to perform an operation any time a window becomes the main. We will register our client object as an observer as shown in Listings 6-1 (Objective-C) and 6-2 (Swift).

Listing 6-1. Objective-C: Registering for a local notification

```
[[NSNotificationCenter defaultCenter] addObserver:self
selector:@selector(windowBecomeMain:) name:NSWindowDidBecomeMai
nNotification object:nil];
```

Listing 6-2. Swift: Registering for a local notification

```
NotificationCenter.default.addObserver(self, selector:
#selector(windowBecomeMain(notif:)), name:NSWindow.
didBecomeMainNotification , object: nil)
```

In this example, the client object is notified when any object posts an NSWindowDidBecomeMainNotification notification.

Registering for Distributed Notifications

An object registers itself to receive a notification by sending the add Observer:selector:name:object:suspensionBehavior: method to an NSDistributedNotificationCenter object, specifying the message the notification center should send, the name of the notification it wants to receive, the identifying string to match, and the behavior to follow if the notification delivery is suspended.

Because the posting object and the observer may be in different processes, notifications can't contain pointers to arbitrary objects. Therefore, the NSDistributedNotificationCenter class requires notifications to use an NSString/String object as the object argument. Notification matching is done based on this string rather than an object pointer.

When a process is no longer interested in receiving notifications immediately, it can suspend the notification delivery. This is often done when the application is hidden or is put into the background. The NSApplication object automatically suspends delivery when the application is not active. The suspensionBehavior argument in the addObserver method identifies how arriving notifications should be handled while delivery is suspended.

There are four different types of suspension behavior as listed in Table 6-1.

Table 6-1. *Distributed notifications: observer's suspension behavior*

Suspension Behavior	Description
NSNotificationSuspensionBehaviorDrop	The server does not queue any notifications with this name and object until it receives the setSuspended:NO message.
NSNotificationSuspensionBehaviorCoalesce	The server queues only the last notification of the specified name and object, i.e., all earlier notifications are dropped.
NSNotificationSuspensionBehaviorHold	The server holds all matching notifications until the queue has been filled (i.e., the queue size is determined by the server) at which point the server may flush queued notifications.

(continued)

Table 6-1. (*continued*)

Suspension Behavior	Description
NSNotificationSuspension BehaviorDeliverImmediately	The server delivers notifications matching this registration irrespective of whether it has received the setSuspended:YES message. When a notification with this suspension behavior is matched, it has the effect of first flushing any queued notifications. The effect is as if the server received setSuspended:NO while the application is suspended, followed by the notification in question being delivered, followed by a transition back to the previous suspended or unsuspended state.

We can suspend notifications by sending setSuspended:YES to the distributed notification center. While notifications are suspended, the notification server handles notifications destined for the process based on the suspension behavior specified by the observers at the time of registering the receive notifications.

When the process resumes the notification delivery, all queued notifications are delivered immediately. In applications using the Application Kit, the NSApplication object automatically suspends the notification delivery when the application is not active.

A notification destined for an observer that registered with NSNotificationSuspensionBehaviorDeliverImmediately automatically flushes the queue as it is delivered, causing all queued notifications to be delivered at that time as well.

The suspended state can be overridden by the originator of the notification. If the notification is urgent, such as a warning of a server being shut down, the originator process can force the notification to be delivered immediately to all observers by posting the notification with the NSDistributedNotificationCenter postNotificationName:object:userInfo:d eliverImmediately: method with the deliverImmediately argument YES.

Refer to Listing 6-3 for Objective-C code and Listing 6-4 for Swift code.

Listing 6-3. Objective-C: Registering for a distributed notification

```
[[NSDistributedNotificationCenter defaultCenter]
addObserver:self selector:@selector(receivedNotification: )
name:NotificationName object:NotificationObject];
```

Listing 6-4. Swift: Registering for a distributed notification

```
DistributedNotificationCenter.default().addObserver(self,
selector: #selector(windowBecomeMain(notif:)), name:
NSNotification.Name(rawValue: "NotificationName"), object:
"NotificationObject", suspensionBehavior: .deliverImmediately)
```

Unregistering an Observer

Before an object that is observing notifications is deallocated, it must tell the notification center to stop sending it notifications. We can send the message listed in Listings 6-5 (Objective-C) and 6-6 (Swift) to completely remove an object as an observer of local notifications, regardless of how many objects and notifications for which it registered itself.

It is also possible to remove the observer status of the object for a particular notification. We will see that later.

Listing 6-5. Objective-C: Remove observer

```
//For local notifications
[[NSNotificationCenter defaultCenter] removeObserver:self];
//For Distributed notifications
[[NSDistributedNotificationCenter defaultCenter]
removeObserver:self];
```

Listing 6-6. Swift: Remove observer

```
//For local notifications
NotificationCenter.default.removeObserver(self)
//For Distributed notifications
DistributedNotificationCenter.default().removeObserver(self)
```

For removing the observer status of any object for a specific notification, use more specific removeObserver methods that specify the notification name and observed object respectively, to selectively unregister an object for particular notifications as shown in the following listings. You should remove object from the observer role before releasing it.

Refer to Listing 6-7 for Objective-C code and Listing 6-8 for Swift code.

Listing 6-7. Objective-C: Remove the observer for a particular notification

```
//For local notifications
[NSNotificationCenter removeObserver:self forKeyPath:
NSWindowDidBecomeMainNotification];
//For Distributed notifications
[NSDistributedNotificationCenter removeObserver:self
forKeyPath:@"NotificationName"];
```

Listing 6-8. Swift: Remove the observer for a particular notification

```
//For local notifications
NotificationCenter.default.removeObserver(self, name:
NSWindow.didBecomeMainNotification, object: nil)
//For Distributed notifications
DistributedNotificationCenter.default().removeObserver(self,
name: NSNotification.Name(rawValue: "NotificationName"),
object: "NotificationObject")
```

IPC Using Distributed Notifications

First, create two new projects in Xcode, each with a macOS App template as shown in Figure 5-10 in Chapter 5. Name them ClientApp and ServerApp, and at this time, you can select whether you want to use Objective-C or Swift as shown in Figure 5-11 in Chapter 5.

Let's look at a simple code to send and receive a distributed notification. Listings 6-9 (Objective-C) and 6-10 (Swift) list the common constants for ServerApp and ClientApp projects. You can put these constants in a header file which will be exposed to the class where you will be writing the code for sending and receiving the notifications.

Listing 6-9. Objective-C: Common to the server and the client

```
#define NotificationName    @"Notification from ServerApp"
#define NotificationObject  @"com.testnotif.com"
```

Listing 6-10. Swift: Common to the server and the client

```
let notificationName =   "Notification from ServerApp"
let notificationObject = "com.testnotif.com"
```

Server Implementation

In the ServerApp project, inside the ViewController class, for example, create a function to send a dictionary in a distributed notification. Refer to Listing 6-11 for Objective-C code and Listing 6-12 for Swift code.

You can write this code in any of your custom classes, and it need not be the default ViewController which comes with the template of the macOS App of the Xcode project. For simplicity of the sample, I am writing this code in ViewController.swift or ViewController.m depending if your project is created for Swift or Objective-C.

Listing 6-11. Objective-C: Send a notification

```
- (void)sendNotification
{
NSDictionary* itemTobeSent = [NSDictionary dictionaryWith
ObjectsAndKeys:@"Notification sent",@"key", nil];
[[NSDistributedNotificationCenter defaultCenter] postNot
ificationName:NotificationName object:NotificationObject
userInfo:itemTobeSent options:NSNotificationDeliverImmediately];
}
```

Listing 6-12. Swift: Send a notification

```
func sendNotification()
{
    let itemTobeSent = ["key" : "Notification sent"]
    DistributedNotificationCenter.default().post(name:
    NSNotification.Name(rawValue: notificationName), object:
    notificationObject, userInfo: itemTobeSent)
}
```

Client Implementation

In the ClientApp project, inside the ViewController class, for example, create a function to receive the distributed notification. Refer to Listing 6-13 for Objective-C code and Listing 6-14 for Swift code.

Again, you can write this code in any of your custom classes, and it need not be the default ViewController which comes with the template of the macOS App of the Xcode project.

First, we will register our intended class as the observer for the distributed notification as listed in Listings 6-3 and 6-4.

Next, we will write a function to receive the notification dispatched by ServerApp.

Listing 6-13. Objective-C: Receive a notification

```
-(void)receivedNotification: (NSNotification*)notification
{
    NSLog(@"received notification :
    %@",[notification.userInfo objectForKey:@"key"]);

    //Do something with received dictionary.
}
```

Listing 6-14. Swift: Receive a notification

```
func receivedNotification(notification : Notification)
{
    print("\(notification.userInfo)")
    //Do something with received dictionary
}
```

It's that simple to implement IPC using distributed notifications.

Time to Run the Code!

To test run, first launch the client app. It will register for the distributed notification. Run the server app, and it will send the notification. The client app will receive the notification, and you can observe the results in the client app's console logs.

Next, we will see how to handle distributed notifications in a multithreading environment.

Delivering Notifications to Threads

Notification centers deliver notifications on the thread in which the notification was posted, but distributed notification centers deliver notifications always on the main thread.

Based on the nature of an application, it may require notifications to be delivered on a particular thread and not on the main thread. For example, if an object in a background thread is listening for notifications from the user interface, such as a window closing, we would like to receive the notifications in the background thread itself rather than on the main thread.

In these cases, we must capture the notifications as they are delivered on the default thread and redirect them to the desired thread.

One way to redirect notifications is to use a custom notification queue to hold any notifications that are received on incorrect threads and then process them on the correct thread.

For this technique to work, we should register for a notification normally. When a notification arrives, we test whether the current thread is the thread that should handle the notification.

If it is the wrong thread, store the notification in a queue and then send a signal to the correct thread, indicating that a notification needs processing.

The other thread receives the signal, removes the notification from the queue, and processes the notification.

To implement this technique, the observer object needs to have instance variables for the following values:

- A mutable array to hold the notifications

- A communication port for signaling the correct thread

- A lock to prevent multithreading conflicts with the notification array

- An NSThread object that identifies the correct thread

We also need methods to set up the variables, to process the notifications, and to receive the Mach messages.

Pros and Cons of IPC Using Distributed Notifications

At times, when tight coupling between two objects is undesirable, notifications can play a vital role in implementing a loosely coupled architecture.

The object posting the notification, the object included in the notification, and the observer of the notification might be the same object or all be different objects. Objects posting the notifications need not know anything about the observers.

Any number of objects can receive the notification, not just the delegate object.

An object can receive any message by registering for the event name, not just the predefined methods.

The object posting the notification does not need to know the observer exists.

Posting a distributed notification is an expensive operation. The notification gets sent to a system-wide server that then broadcasts it to all the processes that have objects registered for distributed notifications.

The latency between posting the notification and the notification's arrival is unbounded. It is possible that, when too many notifications are posted and the server's queue fills up, notifications may be dropped.

Distributed notifications are delivered via a task's run loop. A task must be running a run loop in one of the "common" modes, like NSDefaultRunLoopMode, to receive a distributed notification.

For multithreaded applications running on Mac OS 10.3 and later, distributed notifications are always delivered on the main thread. We need to do extra work to make sure that a notification is received by the concerned thread in a multithreading environment.

NSDistributedNotificationCenter also does not implement a secure communications protocol. When using distributed notifications, your app should not by default trust any data passed in the notification and treat it as untrusted.

Real-World Scenarios for IPC Using Distributed Notifications

Notifications are advisable when you need to subscribe for events occurring with multiple objects. Multiple subscriptions will trigger the responding selector multiple times. But when unsubscribing, all observer selectors will be removed.

Another interesting aspect where you should consider notifications is when you want to do a bulk subscription. One of the interesting features of NotificationCenter is the ability to subscribe for all notifications from a certain object for a certain notification from all objects or basically for all notifications in the notification center.

What's Next?

This is all about IPC using distributed notifications. In the next chapter, we will discuss pasteboards. So, stay tuned and enjoy coding!

CHAPTER 7

IPC Through Pasteboards

The pasteboard server is shared by all running apps. It contains data that the user has cut or copied, as well as other data that one application wants to transfer to another.

NSPasteboard objects are the only interface to the server for an application and to all pasteboard operations.

An NSPasteboard object is also used to transfer data between apps and service providers listed in each application's Services menu.

For transferring data with drag and drop, the drag pasteboard is used to transfer data that is being dragged by the user.

A pasteboard can contain multiple items. We can directly write or read any object that implements the NSPasteboardWriting or NSPasteboardReading protocol, respectively.

This allows us to write and read common items such as URLs, colors, images, strings, attributed strings, and sounds without an intermediary object.

Custom classes can also implement these protocols for use with the pasteboard.

Writing methods provide a convenient means of writing to the first pasteboard item, without having to create the first pasteboard item.

© Hem Dutt 2021
H. Dutt, *Interprocess Communication with macOS*,
https://doi.org/10.1007/978-1-4842-7045-5_7

The general pasteboard, available by way of the general class method, automatically participates with the Universal Clipboard feature in Mac OS 10.12 and later.

IPC Using Pasteboard

A pasteboard is a standard way to exchange data between applications. The most common example of IPC using a pasteboard is copy-paste functionality provided by macOS.

When a user copies the data, it gets placed in the pasteboard, and when the user pastes it, the data is made available to the application from the pasteboard.

Another common example of IPC through a pasteboard is drag and drop features supported by some applications.

Pasteboards exist in a special global memory separate from application processes. A pasteboard object accesses this shared repository where reader and writer applications read or write, respectively.

When moving data between two different applications, the memory space assigned for a pasteboard gets involved, so the data persists even in the absence of the source.

A pasteboard could be public or private depending on the use case. A private pasteboard is recommended if IPC is to be implemented only between predefined client-server apps. If we have to provide a generic copy-paste or drag feature, we need to use public pasteboards.

Let's see an example of IPC using copy/paste of a string through a private pasteboard.

First, create two projects with the macOS App template as shown in Figures 5-10 and 5-11 in Chapter 5.

Objective-C Implementation

Listing 7-1 declares the pasteboard name which is common for server and client apps.

Listing 7-1. Common to both server and client

```
#define PrivatePasteboard @"PrivatePasteboard"
```

Now we will look into the code to write to the pasteboard from a **server** application (Listing 7-2).

Listing 7-2. Writer code

```
- (void)copyToPrivatePasteboard
{
        NSPasteboard* privatePateboard = [NSPasteboard
        pasteboardWithName:PrivatePasteboard];
        //Clear pasteboard from previously copied items
        [privatePateboard clearContents];
        //Create a array of objects that needs to be copied
        //I have used a hard-coded string for example. It
        could be a input from UI
        NSArray* objectTobeCopied = [NSArray
        arrayWithObject:@"IPC using private pasteboard"];
        //Write array of objects to pasteboard
        [privatePateboard writeObjects:objectTobeCopied];
}
```

Next, we will look into the reader code for the **client** application. So, the client will gain access to the private pasteboard by name and will read the copied values (Listing 7-3).

Listing 7-3. Reader code

```
- (void)readFromPrivatePasteboard
{
        NSPasteboard* privatePateboard = [NSPasteboard
        pasteboardWithName:PrivatePasteboard];
        //Specify the type of objects to be read from
        pasteboard
        NSArray *typeArray = [NSArray
        arrayWithObject:[NSString class]];
        NSDictionary *optionsDic = [NSDictionary dictionary];
        //Check if objects of specified type can be read from
        pasteboard
        BOOL canRead = [privatePateboard canReadObjectFor
        Classes:typeArray options:optionsDic];
        if (canRead)
        {
                NSArray *objectsToPaste = [privatePateboard
                readObjectsForClasses:typeArray
                options:optionsDic];
                NSLog(@"%@",objectsToPaste);
        }
}
```

Reading/Writing Custom Data

We might want to read/write a custom object to the pasteboard. This is also possible if the custom object conforms to the NSPasteboardWriting and NSPasteboardReading protocols. Let's understand with one example how it can be done. First, let's declare an interface for the custom object (Listing 7-4).

Listing 7-4. Interface

```
#import <Cocoa/Cocoa.h>
@interface CustomItem : NSObject<NSPasteboardWriting,
NSPasteboardReading>

@property (atomic)    NSInteger objectId;
@property (atomic, strong)    NSString *text;

@end
```

In the implementation file, first synthesize properties "objectId" and "text" as shown in Listing 7-5.

Listing 7-5. Synthesize properties in the implementation

```
@implementation CustomItem
@synthesize objectId;
@synthesize text;
@end
```

Now we will implement pasteboard delegate functions in the implementation file. Listing 7-6 shows the implementation for write support for the **server**, whereas Listing 7-7 shows the implementation for read support for the **client**.

Listing 7-6. Delegate functions for write support

```
#pragma mark -
#pragma mark NSPasteboardWriting support

- (NSArray *)writableTypesForPasteboard:(NSPasteboard *)
pasteboard
{
        // These are the types we can write.
```

```
        NSArray *types = [NSArray arrayWithObjects:
        NSPasteboardTypeString, nil];
        return types;
}

- (NSPasteboardWritingOptions)writingOptionsForType:(NSString
*)type pasteboard:(NSPasteboard *)pasteboard
{
        return 0;
}

- (id)pasteboardPropertyListForType:(NSString *)type
{
        return [NSString stringWithFormat:@"%ld , %@ ",
        self.objectId, self.text];
}
```

Listing 7-7. Delegate functions for read support

```
#pragma mark -
#pragma mark  NSPasteboardReading support

+ (NSArray *)readableTypesForPasteboard:(NSPasteboard *)
pasteboard
{
        return [NSArray arrayWithObjects:(id)kUTTypeURL,
        NSPasteboardTypeString, nil];
}

+ (NSPasteboardReadingOptions)readingOptionsForType:(NSString
*)type pasteboard:(NSPasteboard *)pasteboard
{
        if ([type isEqualToString:NSPasteboardTypeString] ||
        UTTypeConformsTo((__bridge CFStringRef)type, kUTTypeURL))
```

```
        {
                return NSPasteboardReadingAsString;
        }
        else
        {
                return NSPasteboardReadingAsData;
        }
}
```

Now, as shown in Listing 7-8, create an initializer for the class.

Listing 7-8. Initializer

```
- (id)initWithPasteboardPropertyList:(id)propertyList
ofType:(NSString *)type
{
        if ([type isEqualToString:NSPasteboardTypeString])
        {
                self = [super init];
                NSArray* prArr = [propertyList
                componentsSeparatedByString:@","];
                self.objectId = [[prArr objectAtIndex:0]
                integerValue];
                self.text = [prArr objectAtIndex:1];
        }
        else
        {
                NSAssert(NO, @"internal error: type not
                supported");
        }
        return self;
}
```

Swift Implementation

First, declare a pasteboard name to be used by server and client apps (Listing 7-9).

Listing 7-9. Common to both server and client

```
let privatePasteboardName = "PrivatePasteboard"
```

Now we will look into the code to write to the pasteboard from a server application (Listing 7-10).

Listing 7-10. Writer code

```
func copyToPrivatePasteboard()
{
    //Pasteboard
    let privatePasteboard = NSPasteboard(name: NSPasteboard.
    Name(rawValue: privatePasteboardName))
    //Clear pasteboard from previously copied items
    privatePasteboard.clearContents()
    //Create a array of objects that needs to be copied
    //I have used a hard-coded string for example. It could be
    a input from UI
    let objectTobeCopied : [NSPasteboardWriting] = ["IPC using
    private pasteboard" as NSPasteboardWriting]
    //Write array of objects to pasteboard
    privatePasteboard.writeObjects(objectTobeCopied)
}
```

Next, we will look into the reader code for the client application. So, the client will gain access to the private pasteboard by name and will read the copied values (Listing 7-11).

Listing 7-11. Reader code

```
func pasteFromPrivatePasteboard()
{
    //Pasteboard
    let privatePasteboard = NSPasteboard(name: NSPasteboard.
    Name(rawValue: privatePasteboardName))
    let objects = privatePasteboard.readObjects(forClasses:
    [NSString.self], options: nil)
    print(objects as Any)
}
```

Reading/Writing Custom Data

We might want to read/write a custom object to the pasteboard. This is also possible if the custom object conforms to the NSPasteboardWriting and NSPasteboardReading protocols. Let's understand with one example how it can be done. Create a class for the custom object and implement the pasteboard delegate functions (Listing 7-12).

Listing 7-12. Custom data in the pasteboard

```
class CustomItem : NSObject, NSPasteboardWriting,
NSPasteboardReading
{
    var objectId : Int?
    var text : String?
```

```swift
func writableTypes(for pasteboard: NSPasteboard) ->
[NSPasteboard.PasteboardType]
{
    // These are the types we can write.
    let types = [NSPasteboard.PasteboardType.string]
    return types
}

func pasteboardPropertyList(forType type: NSPasteboard.
PasteboardType) -> Any?
{
    return "\(objectId!),\(text!)"
}

static func readableTypes(for pasteboard: NSPasteboard) ->
[NSPasteboard.PasteboardType]
{
    return [NSPasteboard.PasteboardType.string]
}

required init?(pasteboardPropertyList propertyList: Any,
ofType type: NSPasteboard.PasteboardType)
{
    super.init()
    if type == NSPasteboard.PasteboardType.
    string, let prArr = (propertyList as? String)?.
    components(separatedBy: ",")
    {
        objectId = Int(prArr.first!)!
        text = prArr.last!
    }
    else
    {
```

```
                print("internal error: type not supported")
        }
    }
}
```

Time to Run the Code!

Run the server app first to write some data into the pasteboard. Then run the client app to read the data from the pasteboard. The client app should be able to read the content written by the server app.

With this, we are done with the implementation of IPC using pasteboards. Next, let's check the pros and cons of IPC using pasteboards.

Pros and Cons of IPC Using Pasteboards

Whenever we copy-paste a text from a document into another document, we perform IPC using pasteboards. It is a hassle-free way to copy some data from one location to another.

With the feature of creating private pasteboards and the ability to store custom objects in them, it gives a great flexibility for implementing a custom copy-paste from one application to another application sharing the private pasteboard.

Another biggest advantage is that a pasteboard server resides outside an application's process, and so a value copied into the pasteboards remains there even if the application which copied the content quits.

The client application can read the copied data from the pasteboard even when the originating application is not running.

On the other hand, the disadvantage is that the client did not get any notification about the data being available in the pasteboard. The client needs to check the data in the desired pasteboard, and that means this IPC technique is more suitable where data is read and written on specific commands from the client and the server like copy/cut and paste operations.

Real-World Scenarios for IPC Using Pasteboards

As discussed earlier, whenever we copy-paste a text from a document into another document, we perform IPC using pasteboards. Other examples include operations such as copy-pasting a file/image from one location to another location or into an application.

We can also use pasteboards where we need the application to read data which was dragged from a location or from within other applications and dropped on the concerned application.

What's Next?

This is all about IPC using pasteboards. In the next chapter, we will discuss IPC using XPC. So, stay tuned and enjoy coding!

CHAPTER 8

IPC Through XPC

So far, we have discussed many IPC techniques for macOS. The latest is XPC which we are going to discuss in this chapter. Before XPC, a common way to use IPC, and provide services between processes, was through Sockets, Mach messages, or distributed objects.

Apple now encourages developers to use XPC in applications and frameworks that provide services. Also, Apple has updated many of its frameworks, daemons, and applications to use XPC.

XPC provides us with a new level of abstraction for IPC. But aside from providing an easier to use IPC mechanism, XPC also gives us some additional benefits that we will discuss later in this chapter.

Introduction to XPC

The XPC Services API is a part of libSystem which provides a lightweight mechanism for IPC integrated with Grand Central Dispatch (GCD) and launchd. The XPC Services API allows us to create lightweight helper tools, also known as XPC services, that perform work for your application.

There are two main reasons to use XPC services which are discussed as follows.

© Hem Dutt 2021
H. Dutt, *Interprocess Communication with macOS*,
https://doi.org/10.1007/978-1-4842-7045-5_8

Stability

To be honest, applications sometimes can crash. We hate it when this happen, but we have to face it now and then. Often, certain parts of an application are more prone to crashes than others. For example, in a plug-in-based architecture, the stability of an application is inherently at the mercy of the authors of plug-ins.

When one module of an application is at more risk for crash, it can be helpful and intelligent to keep the potentially unstable functionality out from the core of the application. This separation lets us ensure that if a module crashes, the rest of the application is not affected.

Privilege Separation

An application during its lifetime can be exposed to untrusted data based on the nature of the application, such as web pages, files sent by email, and so on. This represents a growing attack vulnerability from viruses and other malware.

With traditional applications, if an application becomes compromised through a buffer overflow or other security vulnerabilities, the attacker gains the ability to do anything that the user can do. To mitigate this risk, macOS provides sandboxing, thus limiting the types of operations a process can perform.

In a sandboxed environment, we can further increase security with privilege separation and divide an application into smaller pieces that are responsible for a part of the application's behavior. This allows each module to have a more restrictive sandbox than the application as a whole.

There are other mechanisms available as well for dividing an application into smaller parts, such as NSTask and posix_spawn, but they do not let us put each module of the application in its own sandbox, so implementing privilege separation is not possible with them. Each

XPC service has its own sandbox, so XPC services can make it easier to implement proper privilege separation.

Architecture and Behavior of XPC

XPC services are managed by launchd, which launches them on demand, restarts them if they crash, and terminates them when they are idle. This is transparent to the application using the service, except when a service crashes while processing a message that requires a response. In this case, the application can see that its XPC connection has become invalid until the service is restarted by launchd. As an XPC service can be terminated suddenly at any time, it must be designed to hold a minimal state; ideally, your service should be completely stateless.

By default, XPC services are run in the most restricted environment, that is, sandboxed with minimal filesystem access, network access, and so on. **Elevating a service's privileges to root is not supported.** Also, an XPC service is private and is available only to the main application that contains it.

There could be times when we would require privilege elevation. We will deal with this topic separately in advanced topics.

On Mac OS 10.8 onward, there are two APIs available for working with XPC services.

NSXPCConnection API

This is an Objective-C-based API that provides a remote procedure call mechanism, allowing the client application to call methods on proxy objects that transparently relay those calls to corresponding objects in the service helper and vice versa.

It consists of classes listed in Table 8-1.

Table 8-1. *NSXPCConnection API*

Classes	Description
NSXPCConnection	This class represents the bidirectional communication channel between client and server processes. Both the application and the service helper must have at least one connection object.
NSXPCInterface	This class describes the expected programmatic behavior of the connection like what classes can be transmitted across the connection, what objects are exposed, etc.
NSXPCListener	This class listens for incoming XPC connections. The service helper must create one of these and assign it a delegate object that conforms to the NSXPCListenerDelegate protocol.
NSXPCListener Endpoint	This class uniquely identifies an NSXPCListener instance and can be sent to a remote process using NSXPCConnection. This allows a process to construct a direct communication channel between two other processes that otherwise are not known to each other.

To use the NSXPCConnection API, we must create the following:

- **An interface**: This mainly consists of a protocol that describes what methods should be exposed from the remote process.

- A connection object on both sides.

- **A listener**: This code in the XPC service accepts connections.

- Messages.

Figure 8-1 shows the structure of the communication between an application and NSXPCConnection.

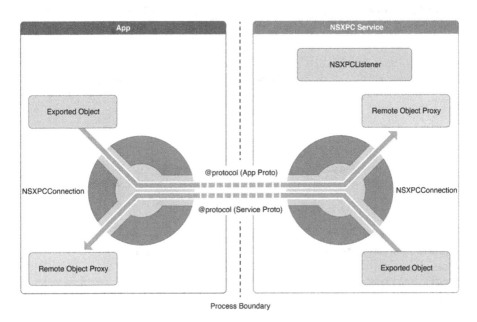

Figure 8-1. *NSXPC architecture (source: developer.apple.com)*

The NSXPCConnection API takes advantage of Objective-C protocols to define the programmatic interface between the service and the calling application. Any instance method that needs to be exposed to the opposite side of a connection must be explicitly defined in a formal protocol.

Figure 8-2 shows the basic steps in creating a communication channel using NSXPCConnection.

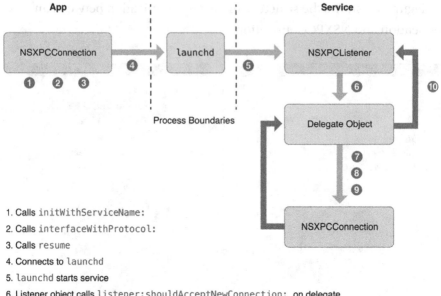

1. Calls initWithServiceName:
2. Calls interfaceWithProtocol:
3. Calls resume
4. Connects to launchd
5. launchd starts service
6. Listener object calls listener:shouldAcceptNewConnection: on delegate
7. Sets exportedObject
8. Sets exportedInterface
9. Calls resume
10. Returns YES

Figure 8-2. *NSXPC connection process (source: developer.apple.com)*

For the implementation example, we will focus on NSXPCConnection only and will touch base on the XPC Services API for only the theoretical purpose.

XPC Services API

The XPC Services API is a C-based API that provides basic messaging services between a client application and a service helper.

The XPC Services API is recommended when you need compatibility with Mac OS 10.7 or if your application and its service are not based on the Foundation framework. The NSXPCConnection API is recommended for apps based on the Foundation framework in Mac OS 10.8 and later.

The XPC Services API has two main building blocks as listed in Table 8-2.

Table 8-2. *XPC Services API*

Classes	Description
xpc.h APIs	These are used for creating and manipulating property list objects and APIs that daemons use to reply to messages.
	This API is at the libSystem level and thus does not depend on Core Foundation. XPC supports connection types such as file descriptors in its object graphs format.
	The XPC API uses its own container that supports only the primitives that are practical to transport across process boundaries because not all CF types can be shared across process boundaries.
connection.h APIs	These are used for connecting to an XPC service. This service is a special helper bundle embedded in an app's bundle.
	A connection is independent of whether an actual instance of the service binary is running. The service binary is launched on demand.
	A connection can also be sent as a piece of data in an XPC message. Hence, you can pass a connection through XPC to allow one service to communicate with another service.

Creating XPC Service

An XPC service is a bundle in the **Contents/XPCServices** directory of the main application bundle. The XPC service bundle contains an Info.plist file, an executable, and any resources needed by the service. The XPC service indicates which function to call when the service receives messages by calling the function listed in Listing 8-1 from its main function.

Listing 8-1. xpc_main

```
func xpc_main(_ handler: xpc_connection_handler_t) -> Never
```

To create an XPC service in Xcode, do the following:

1. Create a new macOS application project in Xcode
   with the name "XPCSampleObjC" as shown in
   Figure 8-3.

Figure 8-3. *Create a Cocoa application*

2. Add a new target to your project by clicking the +
   icon as shown in Figure 8-4. Choose the XPC Service
   template as shown in Figure 8-5.

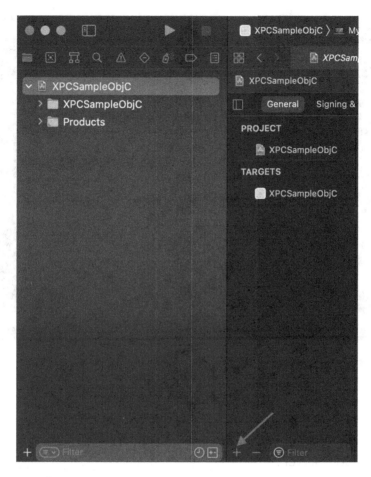

Figure 8-4. *Create a new target*

Figure 8-5. *Create an XPC Service*

3. We will name this new target as "XPCServer"
    (Figure 8-6). This will add one more target
    alongside the main application target with the name
    "XPCServer".

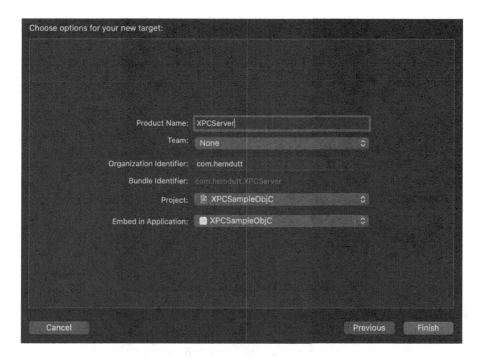

Figure 8-6. *XPCServer*

4. This will create a subproject named "XPCServer" as
    shown in Figure 8-7.

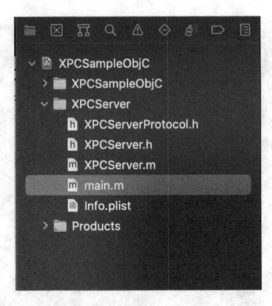

Figure 8-7. *XPCServer subproject*

5. Select the "XPCSampleObjC" target and verify the
    "Embed XPC Services" as shown in Figure 8-8. If you
    do not find this entry, add a Copy Files phase to your
    application's build settings, as shown in Figure 8-8, to
    copy the XPC service into the Contents/XPCServices
    directory of the main application bundle.

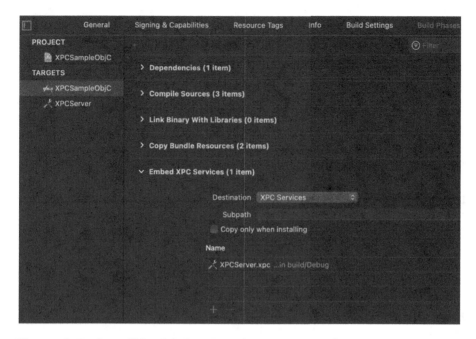

Figure 8-8. *Install in the Contents/XPCServices directory*

6. Again, verify under dependencies that XPCServer is added as a dependency (Figure 8-9). If you don't find this entry, add a dependency to the application's build settings, to indicate it depends on the XPC service bundle as shown in Figure 8-9.

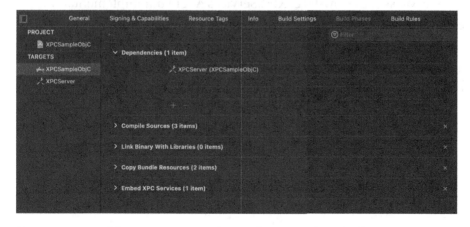

Figure 8-9. *Add a service as a dependency in the app's target*

195

7. If you are writing a low-level (C-based) XPC service, in the main.m file of the XPCServer subproject, implement a minimal main function to register your event handler, as shown in Listing 8-2. Replace my_ event_handler with the name of your event handler function.

Listing 8-2. xpc_main

```
int main(int argc, const char *argv[])
{
    xpc_main(my_event_handler);

    // The xpc_main() function never returns.
    exit(EXIT_FAILURE);
}
```

IPC Using XPC

In our sample applications for performing IPC using XPC, we will look into the Objective-C and Swift implementation based on NSXPCConnection only.

We will skip the low-level XPC Services API in our implementation examples as it is generally not desired to use for Mac OS 10.8 onward.

The NSXPCConnection API is an Objective-C-based API that provides a remote procedure call mechanism. So, first, we will look into the Objective-C implementation for IPC using XPC.

Objective-C Implementation

When working with NSXPCConnection-based server/helper (here, the NSXPCConnection-based app can provide functionality on behalf of the main application, therefore referred to as a helper) apps, both the main application and the server have an instance of NSXPCConnection.

The main application creates its connection object, which causes the server to launch. A delegate method in the server gets passed its connection object when the connection is established.

Each NSXPCConnection object provides the following key features:

- An exported Interface to describe the methods that should be made available to the opposite side of the connection

- An exported Object that contains a local object to handle method calls coming from the other side of the connection

- The ability to obtain a proxy object for calling methods on the other side of the connection

When the main application calls a method on a proxy object, that is, an object residing inside a server, the XPC service's NSXPCConnection object calls that method on the object stored in its exported Object.

Similarly, if the XPC service obtains a proxy object and calls a method on that object, the main app's NSXPCConnection object calls that method on the object stored in its exported Object property.

Designing an Interface

The NSXPCConnection API takes advantage of Objective-C protocols to define the interface between the calling application and the service. Any instance method that we want to call from the opposite side of a connection must be explicitly defined in a protocol.

So, first, in our "XPCServer" subproject, in "XPCServerProtocol.h", import the Foundation framework (Listing 8-3) and define interfaces for both processes.

Listing 8-3. Includes

```
#import <Foundation/Foundation.h>
```

Because communication over XPC is asynchronous, all methods in the protocol must return void. If we need to return data, we need to define a reply block like shown in Listing 8-4.

Listing 8-4. Define a protocol

```
// The protocol that this service will vend as its API. This
header file will also need to be visible to the process hosting
the service.
@protocol XPCServerProtocol

// Replace the API of this protocol with an API appropriate to
the service you are vending.
- (void)upperCaseString:(NSString *)aString withReply:(void (^)
(NSString *))reply;

@end
```

A method can have only one reply block. But, as connections are bidirectional, the XPC service server can also reply by calling methods in the interface provided by the main application.

Each method must have a return type of void, and all parameters to methods or reply blocks must be either arithmetic types, BOOL, NSString, C structures, or arrays containing only the preceding types, that is, Objective-C objects that implement the NSSecureCoding protocol.

Note   If a method or its reply block has parameters that are Objective-C collection classes like NSDictionary, NSArray, and so on, and if you need to pass your own custom objects within a collection, you need to explicitly tell XPC to allow that class as a member of that collection parameter.

Implementing Server Interface

To implement the interface design, we will modify the "XPCServer" class in the XPC Server submodule.

In XPCServer.h, we will find the interface declaration for XPCServer as shown in Listings 8-5 and 8-6.

Listing 8-5. Includes

```
#import <Foundation/Foundation.h>
#import "XPCServerProtocol.h"
```

Listing 8-6. Create an interface

```
// This object implements the protocol which we have defined.
It provides the actual behavior for the service. It is
'exported' by the service to make it available to the process
hosting the service over an NSXPCConnection.
@interface XPCServer : NSObject <XPCServerProtocol>

@end
```

In the implementation file, implement the function declared in "XPCServerProtocol" as shown in Listing 8-7.

Listing 8-7. XPCServer implementation

```
#import "XPCServer.h"

@implementation XPCServer

// This implements the example protocol. Replace the body of
this class with the implementation of this service's protocol.
- (void)upperCaseString:(NSString *)aString withReply:(void (^)
(NSString *))reply
{
    NSString *response = [aString uppercaseString];
    reply(response);
}

@end
```

Accepting Connection XPC Server/Helper

When an NSXPCConnection-based helper receives the first message from a connection, the listener delegate's listener:shouldAcceptNewConnecti on: method is invoked with a listener object and a connection object. This method lets us decide whether to accept the connection by returning YES or discard it by returning NO.

The helper receives a connection request when the first actual message is sent and not when the connection object's resume method is invoked.

In addition to making policy decisions, this method must configure the connection object. Assuming the helper decides to accept the connection, it must set the exported Interface and exported Object properties on the connection.

In the main.m class of the "XPCServer" module, import the Foundation framework as shown in Listing 8-8.

Listing 8-8. Includes

```
#import <Foundation/Foundation.h>
#import "XPCServer.h"
```

Now in the main.m file in the "XPCServer" subproject, we find a template of an interface named "ServiceDelegate" conforming to NSXPCListenerDelegate as shown in Listings 8-9 and 8-10.

Listing 8-9. ServiceDelegate interface

```
@interface ServiceDelegate : NSObject <NSXPCListenerDelegate>

@end
```

Listing 8-10. ServiceDelegate implementation

```
@implementation ServiceDelegate

- (BOOL)listener:(NSXPCListener *)listener shouldAcceptNew
Connection:(NSXPCConnection *)newConnection
{
    // This method is where the NSXPCListener configures,
    accepts, and resumes a new incoming NSXPCConnection.

    // Configure the connection.
    // First, set the interface that the exported object
    implements.
    newConnection.exportedInterface = [NSXPCInterface
    interfaceWithProtocol:@protocol(XPCServerProtocol)];

    // Next, set the object that the connection exports. All
    messages sent on the connection to this service will be
    sent to the exported object to handle. The connection
    retains the exported object.
```

```
    XPCServer *exportedObject = [XPCServer new];
    newConnection.exportedObject = exportedObject;

    // Resuming the connection allows the system to deliver
    more incoming messages.
    [newConnection resume];

    // Returning YES from this method tells the system that
    you have accepted this connection. If you want to reject
    the connection for some reason, call -invalidate on the
    connection and return NO.
    return YES;
}
@end
```

In the main function, we find a template for the instantiation of the ServiceDelegate as mentioned in Listing 8-11.

Listing 8-11. main

```
int main(int argc, const char *argv[])
{
    // Create the delegate for the service.
    ServiceDelegate *delegate = [ServiceDelegate new];

    // Set up the one NSXPCListener for this service. It will
    handle all incoming connections.
    NSXPCListener *listener = [NSXPCListener serviceListener];
    listener.delegate = delegate;

    // Resuming the serviceListener starts this service. This
    method does not return.
    [listener resume];
    return 0;
}
```

With this, we come to the end of the XPC server/helper implementation. Now let's look into client-side code.

Client Implementation

Sending messages with NSXPCConnection is as simple as making a method call. When you call the desired method, the corresponding method in the XPC helper is called automatically. That method, in turn, could use the XPC helper's connection object similarly to call a method on the object exported by the main application.

On the client side, I have implemented a very simple interface where there is an NSTextField to enter a lowercase text and an NSButton to invoke a method in the XPC helper to convert the string into uppercase and then return to the client app through a completion block.

In the ViewController class, import Cocoa and XPCServerProtocol as shown in Listing 8-12. I declared an IBOutlet for textField and a function for NSButton to invoke on button press in Listing 8-13.

Listing 8-12. Includes

```
#import <Cocoa/Cocoa.h>
#import "XPCServerProtocol.h"
```

Listing 8-13. ViewController.h

```
@interface ViewController : NSViewController
{
    NSXPCConnection* _connectionToService;
    IBOutlet NSTextField* _textField;
}

- (IBAction)convertToUpperCase:(id)sender;

@end
```

In the ViewController.m class, implement a button action to invoke the XPC helper to convert a lowercase string to an uppercase string as shown in Listing 8-14.

First, get the service name by copying the bundle identifier of the XPCServer target (Figure 8-10).

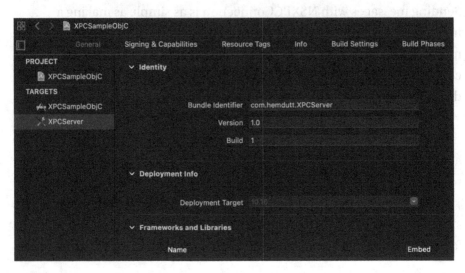

Figure 8-10. *Service name*

Listing 8-14. ViewController.m

```objc
#import "ViewController.h"

@implementation ViewController

- (void)viewDidLoad {
    [super viewDidLoad];

    // Do any additional setup after loading the view.
}
```

```objc
- (IBAction)convertToUpperCase:(id)sender
{

    _connectionToService = [[NSXPCConnection alloc]
    initWithServiceName:@"com.hemdutt.XPCServer"];
    _connectionToService.remoteObjectInterface =
    [NSXPCInterface interfaceWithProtocol:
    @protocol(XPCServerProtocol)];
    [_connectionToService resume];

    [[_connectionToService remoteObjectProxy] upperCaseString:_
    textField.stringValue withReply:^(NSString *aString) {
        // We have received a response. Update our text field,
        but do it on the main thread.
        NSLog(@"Result string was: %@", aString);
        dispatch_async(dispatch_get_main_queue(), ^{
            [self->_textField setStringValue:aString];
            [self->_connectionToService invalidate];
        });
    }];
}

@end
```

With this, we come to the end of implementing IPC using XPC. We have covered the server/helper and client application in Objective-C. Now let's look into the Swift implementation.

Swift Implementation

Almost all new projects and application development are happening in Swift. So, it is almost obvious that we want to use XPC and add an XPC Service to our Swift app. It's a good idea, but a slight problem is that Xcode spits out Objective-C code when you add an XPC Service target.

One way of working through this is to use Objective-C bridging headers. But that means you will have to keep Objective-C code within Swift code. That is not desirable if any other way around is possible. Fortunately, converting Xcode's starter code to Swift is quite straightforward. Let's tweak some setting and make it completely Swift code.

After creating an XPC Service target as shown in Figures 8-5 and 8-6, named "XPCServerSwift," we have four files: main.m, XPCServerSwift.h, XPCServerSwift.m, and XPCServerProtocol.h.

Rename these files to main.swift, XPCServer.swift, XPCServiceDelegate. swift, and XPCServerSwiftProtocol.swift. Next, add them to the target's "Compile Sources" build phase as shown in Figure 8-11.

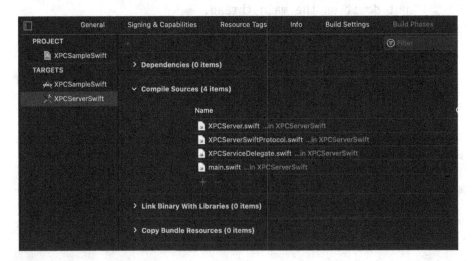

Figure 8-11. *Build phases*

Go to **Build Settings** and perform the following changes:

- **Install Objective-C Compatibility Header**: NO

- **Objective-C Generated Interface Header Name**: ""

- **Runtime Search Paths**: @loader_path/../../../../ Frameworks

- **Swift Language Version**: Whatever version of Swift you use

Please refer to Figures 8-12 to 8-15.

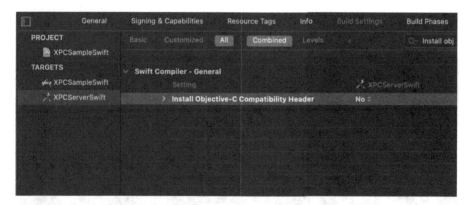

Figure 8-12. *Install Objective-C Compatibility Header*

Figure 8-13. *Swift Language Version*

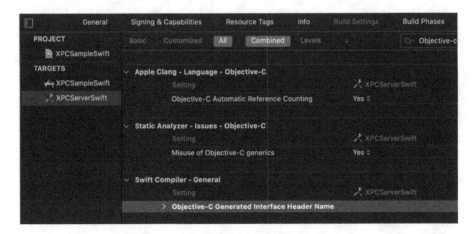

Figure 8-14. *Objective-C Generated Interface Header Name*

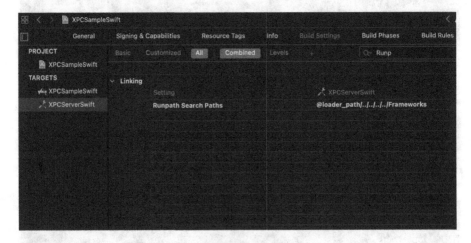

Figure 8-15. *Runtime Search Paths*

Now we will replace the Objective-C code in each file with its Swift translation as shown in Listings 8-15 to 8-18.

Listing 8-15. XPCServerSwiftProtocol.swift

```swift
import Foundation

@objc public protocol XPCServerSwiftProtocol
{
    func upperCaseString(_ string: String, withReply reply:
    @escaping (String) -> Void)
}
```

Listing 8-16. XPCServiceDelegate.swift

```swift
import Foundation

class XPCServiceDelegate: NSObject, NSXPCListenerDelegate
{
    func listener(_ listener: NSXPCListener,
    shouldAcceptNewConnection newConnection: NSXPCConnection)
    -> Bool
    {
        let exportedObject = XPCServer()
        newConnection.exportedInterface = NSXPCInterface(with:
        XPCServerSwiftProtocol.self)
        newConnection.exportedObject = exportedObject
        newConnection.resume()
        return true
    }
}
```

Listing 8-17. XPCServer.swift

```
import Foundation

class XPCServer: NSObject, XPCServerSwiftProtocol
{
    func upperCaseString(_ string: String, withReply reply:
    @escaping (String) -> Void)
    {
        let response = string.uppercased()
        reply(response)
    }
}
```

Listing 8-18. main.swift

```
import Foundation

let delegate = XPCServiceDelegate()
let listener = NSXPCListener.service()
listener.delegate = delegate
listener.resume()
```

With this, we are done with the Swift implementation of the XPC server/helper. Now let's look at the client-side implementation in Swift.

Client Implementation

On the client side, again I have implemented a very simple interface where there is an NSTextField to enter a lowercase text and an NSButton to invoke a method in the XPC helper to convert the string into uppercase and then return to the client app through a completion block.

Let's look at the client-side implementation in Listing 8-19.

Listing 8-19. ViewController.swift

```swift
import Cocoa
import XPCServerSwift

class ViewController: NSViewController
{

    @IBOutlet var textField : NSTextField!

    override func viewDidLoad()
    {
        super.viewDidLoad()

        // Do any additional setup after loading the view.
    }

    @IBAction func converStringToUpperCase(sender : Any?)
    {
        let connection = NSXPCConnection(serviceName: "com.
        hemdutt.XPCServerSwift")
        connection.remoteObjectInterface = NSXPCInterface(with:
        XPCServerSwiftProtocol.self)
        connection.resume()

        let service = connection.
        remoteObjectProxyWithErrorHandler { error in
            print("Received error:", error)
        } as? XPCServerSwiftProtocol

        service?.upperCaseString(textField.stringValue) {
        response in

            print("Response from XPC service:", response)

            DispatchQueue.main.async
```

```
        {
            //Always update UI on main thread
            self.textField.stringValue = response
        }

        connection.invalidate()
    }
  }

}
```

User Interface

In both Objective-C and Swift implementations, on the client side, we created a text field for entering input and a button to execute the XPC service function.

So before building this project, we will go to "Main.storyboard" in the project and add a text field and button on the window as shown in Figure 8-16. Link the IBOutlet of textField and the action of the function "converStringToUpperCase" in the ViewController class to TextField and Button created on the UI, respectively.

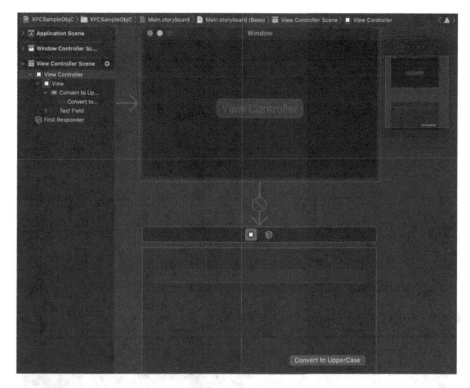

Figure 8-16. *Add a text field and button*

Time to Run the Code!

That's all and we are ready to roll with IPC using XPC in the project. Run
the project. It will open a window with a TextField and a button with the
title "Convert to UpperCase" (Figure 8-17). Enter the input string in a
lower case in the TextField and click the button to convert to an uppercase
string. The uppercase string will be visible in the same TextField on the UI
(Figure 8-18).

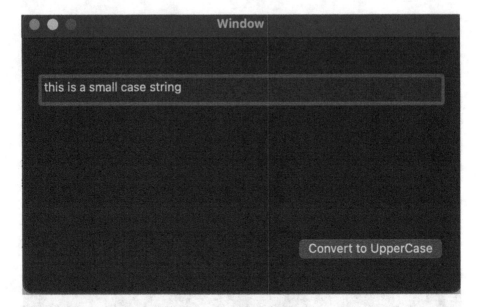

Figure 8-17. *Input a lower case string*

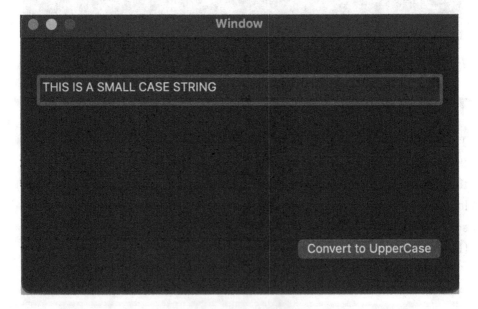

Figure 8-18. *Output an uppercase string*

Next, we will discuss the pros and cons and real-life scenarios where IPC using XPC makes sense.

Pros and Cons of IPC Using XPC

The idea behind XPC is to provide a new abstraction for IPC. The XPC mechanism offers an alternative to sockets or Mach Services for IPC.

But aside from having an easier to use IPC mechanism, the XPC implementation also gives us some additional benefits as discussed in the following.

Imagine we have an application that handles the user's projects. The app provides an API that you could access from your applications and query for details on the user's projects. In this example, the app can be easily modularized using the XPC service.

In another example, if our app wants to access a user's contacts, we can use Contacts.framework which inherently uses the XPC service. We don't need to access the XPC service directly; we use the API provided by Contacts.framework.

XPC services used in this way are an excellent way to communicate different processes. The exchange of data in XPC is through plists, which also allows for data type validation.

Another important advantage is that XPC provides an efficient way to modularize the app in different processes.

When we talk about XPC Services, we are referring to the bundle called the XPC Service. Bundles in Apple macOS refer to entities represented by a specific directory structure.

The most common bundles we come around are application bundles themselves. If we right-click any application and select Show content, we'll find a directory structure.

Applications can have many XPC Service bundles. We can find them inside the Contents/XPCServices/ directory inside the application bundle. You can search in your /Applications directory and see how many of the applications rely on XPC Services.

Using XPC Services in our apps allows us to break some functionality in separate modules. We could create an XPC Service that can be in charge of running some costly but infrequent tasks, for example, some crypto task to generate random numbers or implementing image processing.

Modularizing our application into specific services allows us to keep our main application leaner, and it also takes less memory while running by only running our XPC Service on demand.

Another additional benefit is that the XPC Service runs on its own process. If that process crashes or gets killed, it doesn't affect our main application. Imagine that your application supports user-defined plug-ins built using XPC Services. If they are poorly coded and crash, they won't affect the integrity of your main application.

One more additional advantage to the XPC Service is that they can have their own entitlements. The application will only require the entitlement when it makes use of a service provided by the XPC Service that requires the entitlement.

For example, if you have an app that uses a location but only for specific features, you could move those features to an XPC Service and add the location entitlement only to that XPC Service. If the user never needs the feature that uses the location, it won't be prompted for permissions, making the app more trustworthy.

With traditional applications, if an application becomes compromised through a buffer overflow or other security vulnerabilities, the attacker gains the ability to do anything that the user can do. To mitigate this risk, macOS provides sandboxing, thus limiting the types of operations a process can perform.

These are some of the great benefits of using XPC. Let's see a few downsides of XPC Services as well.

Each XPC service has its own sandbox, so XPC services can make it easier to implement a proper privilege separation. But the downside of this is that we cannot do privilege elevation with sandboxed XPC services.

Real-World Scenarios for IPC Using XPC

Apple recommends and also uses XPC extensively for various parts of the operating system, and a lot of the system frameworks use XPC to implement their functionality. A quick run of the terminal command listed in Listing 8-20 shows numerous XPC services inside frameworks, ranging from Address Book to WebKit.

Listing 8-20. List XPC servises running on system

```
% find /System/Library/Frameworks -name \*.xpc
```

If we do the same search on /Applications, we find apps ranging from the iWork suite to Xcode and even some third-party apps using XPC services.

An excellent example of XPC is within Xcode itself. When we are editing Swift code in Xcode, Xcode communicates with SourceKit over XPC for things such as source code parsing, syntax highlighting, typesetting, and autocomplete.

It's actually also used extensively on iOS by Apple.

What's Next?

During the course of this book, we have come across multiple IPC mechanisms ranging from low-level to high-level abstractions. I hope the journey so far was smooth, and I was able to cover most important aspects in effective manner.

With this chapter, we are close to conclude our journey of IPC on macOS.

In the next chapter, we will explore and implement IPC between a Cocoa application and a web application.

Happy learning and stay tuned for more interesting stuff!

CHAPTER 9

IPC Between Native and Web Apps

Often, during the development of an iOS- or macOS-based application, we come across requirements where the app needs to interact in some way with a web page that is being loaded within the app itself. These requirements could be because that you already have a feature developed on the Web which you want to reuse, or you want to implement a cross-platform feature using a web environment.

Apple provides a WKWebView class to interact with web apps from within the application. A WKWebView object is a view that is used to incorporate web content seamlessly into a native app's UI. WKWebView supports a full web browsing experience and presents HTML, CSS, and JavaScript content alongside an app's native views.

The interaction between native code and WKWebView can help in various aspects while developing an app that loads a web page.

Introduction to WKWebView

WKWebView offers control on the navigation and user experience through a delegate. A navigation delegate reacts when the user clicks links in web content and can interact with the content affecting the navigation. For example, you can prevent a user from navigating to a new content

© Hem Dutt 2021
H. Dutt, *Interprocess Communication with macOS*,
https://doi.org/10.1007/978-1-4842-7045-5_9

till custom conditions are met. A UI delegate on the other hand is used to present native UI elements, such as alerts or contextual menus, in response to interactions with web content.

We can embed a WKWebView object programmatically into an app's view hierarchy or can add it using Interface Builder. Interface Builder provides many customizations, like media playback, configuring data detectors, and interaction behaviors. For more custom customizations, create a web view programmatically using a WKWebViewConfiguration object.

Before a web view appears on the screen, load content from a web server using a URLRequest structure or load content directly from a local file or HTML. The web view automatically loads embedded resources such as videos or images at the initial load request. It then renders content and displays the results inside the view.

You can scale web content the first time it appears in a web view. After that, a user can change the scale using gestures.

WKWebView provides a complete browsing experience, which includes the ability to navigate between different web pages using forward and back buttons, links, and more. When a user clicks a link in web content, the web view acts like a browser and displays the content at that link. To block navigation or to customize your web view's navigation behavior, provide the web view with a navigation delegate conforming to the WKNavigationDelegate protocol. Use the navigation delegate to track the loading progress of new content or to modify the web view's navigation behavior.

You can also use WKWebView APIs to navigate programmatically through the content or to trigger navigation from other parts of the app's interface.

WKWebView also makes it possible for native code to interact with HTML and JavaScript, making it possible to implement IPC between native code and web apps.

IPC Using WKWebView

The WKWebView class can be used to display interactive web content in a macOS app just like an in-app browser. WKWebView is part of the WebKit framework, and it uses the same browser engine as Safari. To be able to use WKWebView in the app, first add WebKit framework in the project. Let's look at the Swift implementation for the same.

Adding a web view to a macOS app is very simple and is similar to adding a UIView or UIButton to your view controller in Interface Builder.

Click and open the Storyboard (for a sample, we can use Main. storyboard, Figure 9-1) for adding the web view in Interface Builder. Open the Object library by clicking the "+" button on the top right as shown in Figure 9-2.

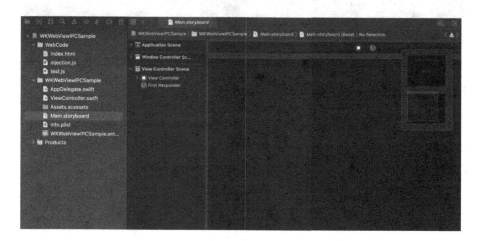

Figure 9-1. *Open Main.storyboard*

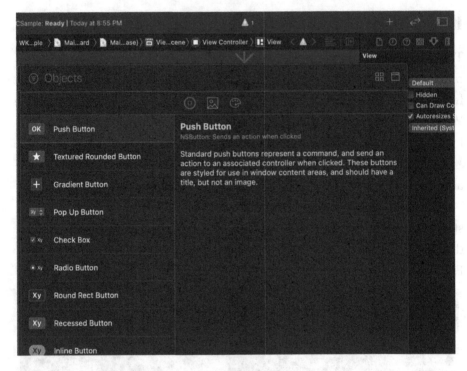

Figure 9-2. *Open the Object library*

Now, we will find the web view or WKWebView in the Object library of
Interface Builder (Figure 9-3). Drag and drop a WKWebView object from
the Object library to your view controller's canvas.

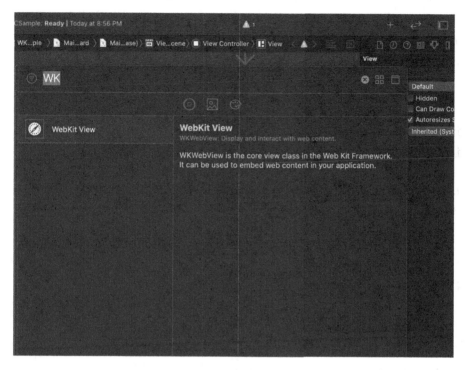

Figure 9-3. *Select a web view*

ViewController class must conform to WKScriptMessageHandler
to adopt a way to respond to JavaScript messages in the web view.
When JavaScript code sends a message that specifically targets the
message handler in the app, WebKit calls the app handler's
userContentController(_:didReceive:) method.

Also, conform ViewController to WKNavigationDelegate to implement
the methods of the WKNavigationDelegate protocol to coordinate
changes in the web view's main frame. In an attempt to navigate web
content, the web view coordinates with its navigation delegate to manage
any transitions. For example, we might use these methods to restrict
navigation from specific links. We can also use these to track the progress
of requests and to respond to authentication challenges and errors. In the

ViewController.swift, import WebKit framework (Listing 9-1) and conform the class to WKScriptMessageHandler and WKNavigat ionDelegate as shown in Listing 9-2.

Listing 9-1. Imports

```
import Cocoa
import WebKit
```

Listing 9-2. Conform with WKScriptMessageHandler and WKNavigationDelegate

```
class ViewController: NSViewController, WKScriptMessageHandler,
WKNavigationDelegate
{

}
```

Create an IBOutlet variable for the WKWebView object and connect to the View Controller as shown in Listing 9-3.

Listing 9-3. WebView object

```
@IBOutlet var webView:WKWebView!
```

Also, we will declare a message name for which we would like to capture events generated from JavaScript from the web app as shown in Listing 9-4.

Listing 9-4. Message name

```
let messageName = "OSXapp"
```

Configuring Web View

Before starting on IPC with WKWebView, we will have to do some configurations as shown in Listing 9-5.

Listing 9-5. Configure a web view

```
func configureWebView()
{
    if #available(OSX 11.0, *)
  {
    let preferences = WKWebpagePreferences()
    preferences.allowsContentJavaScript = true
    webView.configuration.defaultWebpagePreferences =
    preferences
  }
  else
  {
    // Fallback on earlier versions
    let preferences = WKPreferences()
    preferences.javaScriptEnabled = true
    webView.configuration.preferences = preferences
  }
  webView.configuration.userContentController.add(self,
  name: messageName)
    webView.navigationDelegate = self
//Load html file in the web view
    let url = Bundle.main.url(forResource: "index",
    withExtension: "html")
    let request = URLRequest(url: url!)
    webView.load(request)
}
```

WKPreferences aren't really compulsory, but I showed them here to highlight that you can disable JavaScript in the pages you load by setting javaScriptEnabled to false.

But the WKWebViewConfiguration object is necessary if we need to enable the message passing between the web page and native code. By adding self as userContentController, we can receive messages from the page in the view controller itself.

By setting the ViewController class as the WKNavigationDelegate of the web view, we want to know when the page has finished loading, and we want to check the URLs visited by the page. This is an alternate way to communicate from the web page to the code. This was the only way possible for IPC with UIWebViews.

In the last three lines, we have used an HTML file to load in the web view. We will look into the implementation of this HTML file and JavaScript next.

Web Code

Add three new files in the project, "index.html", "injection.js", and "test. js", respectively, as shown in Figure 9-4. We will update these files to implement web code.

Figure 9-4. *Web code*

Let's look at the HTML code first. In "index.html", write code listed in Listing 9-6.

Listing 9-6. index.html

```
<html>
    <head>
        <script charset='UTF-8' type="text/javascript"
        src="test.js"></script>
    </head>
    <body>
        <h1>Test</h1>
        <a href="javascript:void(0)" onclick="sendMessageTo
        Native();">Run sendMessage</a>
        <br><br>
        <a href="javascript:void(0)" onclick="sendMessageWith
        Parameters();">Run sendMessageParameters</a>
    </body>
</html>
```

Next, let's look at the JavaScript code. In the "test.js" file, write code listed in Listing 9-7.

Listing 9-7. test.js

```
function sendMessageToNative()
{
    window.webkit.messageHandlers.OSXapp.
postMessage({parameter1 : "value1", parameter2 : "value2"})
}
```

```
function sendMessageWithParameters()
{
    window.webkit.messageHandlers.OSXapp.postMessage("parameters?
    parameter1=100&parameter2=200&parameter3=abcd")
}

function testEvaluateJavaScript(parameter)
{
    return parameter
}
```

Call JavaScript from Native Code

The method to call a JavaScript function from a native code is similar to what was available in UIWebView. The only difference is that with the UIWebView we had a synchronous call with a String as a return value, whereas WKWebView provides a callback with an error an optional object of type Any returning from the JavaScript function.

If there is an error, we get a description into the error object; else, the response contains what is returned by the function. It could be a String, or it could even be an object, like an array or a dictionary.

For example, we can write code in ViewController to call a JavaScript function "testEvaluateJavaScript" listed in Listing 9-7 when the web view finished the navigation (Listing 9-8).

Listing 9-8. Call JavaScript

```
func webView(_ webView: WKWebView, didFinish navigation:
WKNavigation!)
{
    webView.evaluateJavaScript("testEvaluateJavaScript(true)")
{ (success, result) in
```

```
    if let result = result
    {
        print(result)
    }

    print(success as Any)
  }
}
```

Call Native Code from JavaScript

postMessage listed in Listing 9-7 is the unique method available with the WKWebView. It allows JavaScript to send a message to the native code, and it is also possible to support multiple messages with different handlers in case we need different kinds of messages to be dispatched to different classes on your code.

As we saw in previous listings, an object can be registered to be the handler for a particular message by calling configuration. userContentController.add(self, name: messageName) during the WKWebView configuration.

"OSXapp" is the name of our message added to userContentController, and we can have more of those names if we like. In postMessage, we can send an object as an array or a dictionary. We can also send a string as well in url parameter. A URL with custom scheme even if launched from outside application can be catured and parsed as well.

Also, I checked the message name that could be needed if we register the same object for different messages, so we can handle all the messages in the same place but have different actions for different messages.

Let's see how a macOS app intercepts the message from JavaScript. In the ViewController class, write code as shown in Listing 9-9.

Listing 9-9. Call native code from JavaScript

```
func userContentController(_ userContentController:
WKUserContentController, didReceive message: WKScriptMessage)
{
    if message.name == messageName
    {
        if let body = message.body as? [String:AnyObject]
        {
            print(body)
        }
        else if let body = message.body as? String
        {
            print(body)
        }
    }
}
```

Passing Parameters Through URL

As discussed earlier, there are two ways to communicate from the web page to the native code. The first one we discussed was through WKWebView handlers. The other way is also compatible with now deprecated UIWebView and involves redirecting the page to a URL with a particular scheme with passing parameters into the redirection URL itself similar to a GET request to a web server.

A method of WKNavigationDelegate allows us to block a request from being served or to parse a particular URL. We in theory could block every external URL from a page we are loading into our app or block requests external to a particular domain.

In our sample code in the ViewController class, to keep it simple, we only want to check if there are parameters inside the URL, but only if the URL starts with our prefix "OSXapp" (Listing 9-10).

Listing 9-10. Pass parameters through a URL

```
func webView(_ webView: WKWebView, decidePolicyFor
navigationAction: WKNavigationAction, decisionHandler:
@escaping (WKNavigationActionPolicy) -> Void)

{
    let url = navigationAction.request.url
    if let urlString = url?.absoluteString,
        urlString.starts(with: messageName)
    {
        print(urlString)
    }

    decisionHandler(.allow)
}
```

Time to Run the Code!

Before running the sample code, we will have to do one more thing if your app is sandboxed. Go to target "WKWebViewIPCSample," expand App Sandbox ➤ Network, and check Incoming Connections and Outgoing Connections as shown in Figure 9-5.

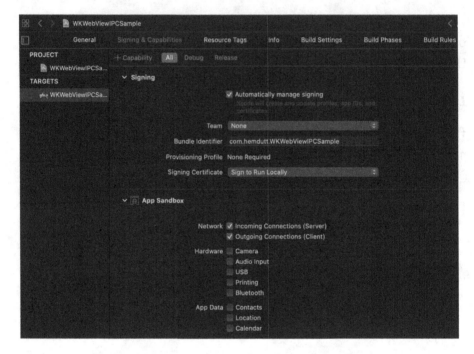

Figure 9-5. *Network connection setting in App Sandbox*

On running the sample code, the app will present a window with HTML content as shown in Figure 9-6. It will show two links "Run sendMessage" and "Run sendMessageParameters." **On click of the links, we can observe the results in console logs.**

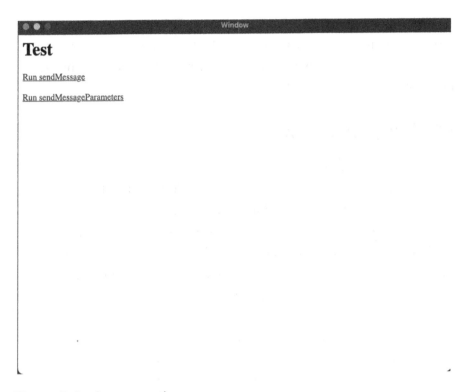

Figure 9-6. *App execution*

On clicking the "Run sendMessage" link, we observe the log in the console as listed in Listing 9-11.

Listing 9-11. Logs after clicking the "Run sendMessage" link

```
["parameter1": value1, "parameter2": value2]
```

On clicking the "Run sendMessageParameters" link, we observe the log in the console as listed in Listing 9-12.

Listing 9-12. Logs after clicking the "Run sendMessageParameters" link

```
parameters?parameter1=100&parameter2=200&parameter3=abcd
```

With this, we come to the end of executing IPC between native and web components within the application. In the next sections, let's discuss the pros and cons and the real-world problems and scenarios using the IPC technique discussed in the chapter.

JavaScript Injection

In all the IPC scenarios of web to native and native to web message passing discussed earlier, all the web code needed for the interaction with the native code and all the code for modifying the web page are already present in the web page source code. In the majority of cases, we need not have access to the server web code and the web page in the native program. But, in some cases, we need the web code to be modular enough that we can inject our custom implementation into the HTML page. This can be achieved with injected interaction or in other words injecting JavaScript from native code to a web page.

Injected interaction is very helpful when the changes on the web page are not advised on the server side or the web page is shared by multiple native apps and provides a skeleton function to be override by native applications as per the design and features. This also comes in handy when the server team denies changes to the concerned web page due to several business or technical reasons.

In this section, we will look into injected interaction where the JavaScript is not included with the HTML page. In this case, we will use the WKUserScript class to implement the JavaScript injection. A WKWebView's configuration property (WKConfiguration) contains a controller object which we will use for injecting JavaScript.

Create another property in ViewController to capture messages generating from a button event on the web page as shown in Listing 9-13.

Listing 9-13. Message name

```
let messageNameEcho = "OSXappEcho"
```

Now we will inject JavaScript named "injection.js" in the HTML page. For that, we will write code listed in Listing 9-14 in the configureWebView() function listed in Listing 9-5.

This code will inject the contents of the "injection.js" file at the start of the document that the WebView will load. Hence, the JavaScript inside the file can be maintained and manipulated as per the required specifications.

Listing 9-14. Inject injection.js

```
// Get the contents of the file `injection.js`
if let filePath:String = Bundle(for: ViewController.self).
path(forResource: "injection", ofType:"js")
{
    do
    {
        let script = try String(contentsOfFile: filePath,
        encoding: .utf8)

        let userScript:WKUserScript =  WKUserScript(source:
        script, injectionTime: WKUserScriptInjectionTime.
        atDocumentStart, forMainFrameOnly: false)
         webView.configuration.userContentController.
         addUserScript(userScript)
    }
    catch let error as NSError
    {
        print(error.localizedDescription)
    }
}
webView.configuration.userContentController.add(self, name:
messageNameEcho)
```

Now, let's look at the "injection.js" implementation at once and update the "injection.js" file with the code in Listing 9-15.

Listing 9-15. injection.js

```
//Echo text entered on Web view
function echoMessage(newText)
{
    var echoElement = document.getElementById("echoElement");
    echoElement.innerText = newText;
}

//Send message to native application
function sendToNative(message)
{
    var native = window.webkit.messageHandlers.OSXappEcho
    native.postMessage(message)
}

//Button press event to send the message to native application
function sendMessage()
{
    var element = document.getElementById("textField");
    console.log(element.value);
    sendToNative(element.value);
    // reset value
    element.value = "";
}
```

We will also need to update our "index.html" file listed in Listing 9-6 to be able to present a text field and button to implement the message echo implementation. Let's see the updated "index.html" in Listing 9-16.

Listing 9-16. index.html

```
<html>
    <head>
        <script charset='UTF-8' type="text/javascript"
        src="test.js"></script>
        </head>
        <body>
            <div class="container">
                <h2> HTML Interaction </h2>
                <p>This is a simple Javascript based web page.
                Values entered in text box will be echoed</p>
                <p id="echoElement">Echo message here.</p>
                <hr/>
                <h3> Native</h3>
                <p>Value entered here will be sent back to
                Native app</p>
                <input id="textField" placeholder="Enter to
                send" class="input"/>
                <button class="button" onclick =
                "sendMessage()" >Send</button>
            </div>
        </body>
    </head>
    <body>
        <h1>Test</h1>
        <a href="javascript:void(0)" onclick="sendMessage
        ToNative();">Run sendMessage</a>
        <br><br>
        <a href="javascript:void(0)" onclick="sendMessageWith
        Parameters();">Run sendMessageParameters</a>
    </body>
</html>
```

We will also need to update the function listed in Listing 9-9 to capture messages with the name "OSXappEcho". In this function, after capturing the message from WebView, we will simply call evaluateJavaScript to echo the message to WebView again. Let's see the updated function in Listing 9-17.

Listing 9-17. Injected interaction

```
func userContentController(_ userContentController:
WKUserContentController, didReceive message: WKScriptMessage)
{
    if message.name == messageName
    {
        if let body = message.body as? [String:AnyObject]
        {
            print(body)
        }
        else if let body = message.body as? String
        {
            print(body)
        }
    }
    else if message.name == messageNameEcho
    {
        if let body = message.body as? String
        {
            webView.evaluateJavaScript("echoMessage
            ('\(body)')") { (success, result) in

                if let result = result
                {
                    print(result)
                }
```

```
            print(success as Any)
        }
    }
    else
    {
        print(message.body)
    }
}
}
```

Time to Run the Code!

After updating the code as described in section "JavaScript Injection," we will see an updated web UI (Figure 9-7) after recompiling and running the code.

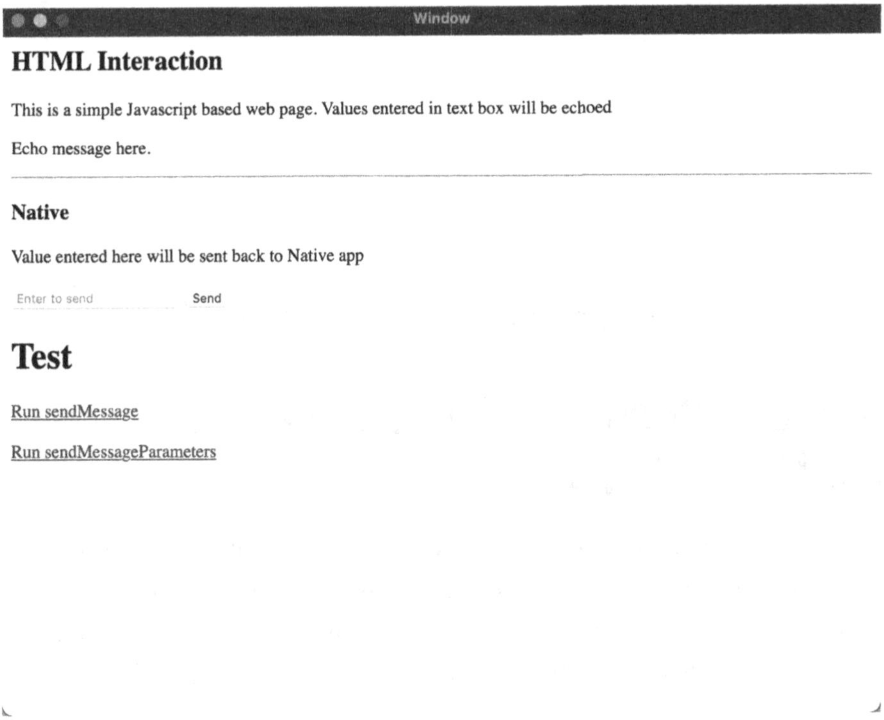

Figure 9-7. Updated web UI

Enter some text (say, "This is a Test String") in the textbox and click the **Send** button. This will send the text to the native app, and it will echo it back to the web page as shown in Figure 9-8.

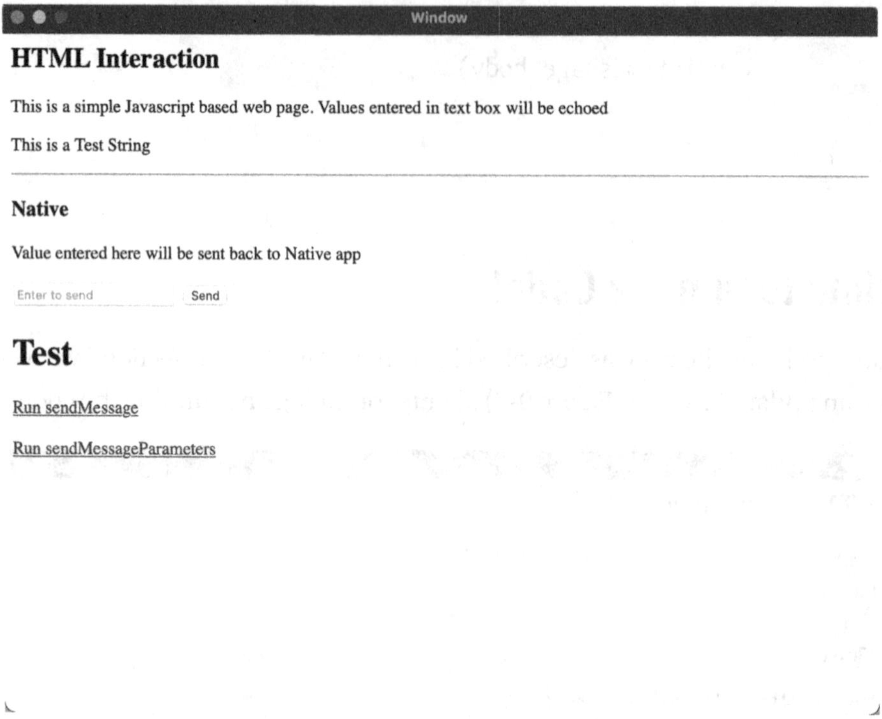

Figure 9-8. *Web page got an echo from the native app*

Pros and Cons of IPC Between Web and Native Apps

WKWebViews are great in displaying web content within the app, thus giving us the capability to "make once and use in multiple apps." But the advantages of WKWebView go beyond displaying web pages in our app. The main advantage of WKWebView is the ability to implement

IPC between web and native applications. Whenever we need in our app to implement a feature which needs us to interact with a website, WKWebView with its IPC capabilities is the choice.

But there are a few limitations as well; when we need to implement authentication using third-party authentication services, WKWebView is not the right choice as most of the third-party authentication services like Google or Akamai do not support WKWebView for their authentication services. In such scenarios, ASWebAuthenticationSession is the recommended way.

Another important aspect of creating a hybrid app is GUI consistency between the web app and the native app. Too much use of web components does not reflect good on the GUI aspect as it hampers the native look and feel on the application.

Real-World Scenarios for IPC Between Native and Web Apps

WKWebView is the pivot of the modern WebKit API introduced in iOS 8 and macOS Yosemite. It replaced UIWebView in UIKit and WebView in AppKit and offered a consistent API across the two platforms.

It boasts a 60fps scrolling responsiveness, streamlined communication between apps and web pages, built-in gestures, and the same JavaScript engine as Safari.

It replaced a single class and protocol, that is, UIWebView and UIWebViewDelegate, with 14 classes and 3 protocols in the WebKit framework, providing an architecture which is much cleaner and allows for a lot of new features.

As WKUserScript allows JavaScript injection at the start or end of the document load, it allows safe and consistent way for web content to be manipulated.

241

There are loads of applications on the App Store and otherwise which use WKWebView for integrating web components within the native application and creating hybrid apps. A lot of products which support multiple platforms like macOS, iOS, Android, the Web, Windows, and so on take advantage of IPC capabilities platforms provide between native and web components, thus reusing the existing web code across multiple platforms.

What's Next?

During our IPC journey so far, we have come across multiple IPC mechanisms ranging from low-level to high-level abstractions and Mach ports to Sockets to Apple Events, and so on.

In this chapter, we discussed how we can achieve IPC between a web app and a native app and thus create a hybrid app which can reuse its web components across multiple platforms.

All these techniques studied so far need a user privilege level but cannot elevate the privilege level to perform tasks beyond the privilege level of the current user.

We will look into the problem of privilege elevation and the associated IPC architecture in the next chapter. Stay tuned!

CHAPTER 10

Privilege Elevation

By default, applications on macOS run with the privileges of the currently logged in user. Different users might have different rights with respect to changing system-wide settings, accessing files, and so on, which depend on whether they are admin users or ordinary users. Majority of tasks on macOS can be executed with admin privileges, but there are a few operations that require additional privileges above and beyond the scope of even an admin user. An application or process having such additional rights is said to be running with elevated privileges. But the elevation of privileges comes with its own drawbacks as running code with root privileges can exponentially increase the dangers posed by security vulnerabilities. In this chapter, we will discuss the risks in privilege elevation and secure ways to privilege elevation.

It is not allowed to elevate privileges for an application submitted to the Mac App Store and also not possible in iOS.

When Do We Need Elevated Privileges?

The following is a list of tasks which require an application to acquire elevated privileges:

1. Manipulating file ownership and permissions

2. Creating, reading, updating, or deleting system files

3. Opening privileged ports (port numbers less than 1024) for TCP and UDP connections

© Hem Dutt 2021
H. Dutt, *Interprocess Communication with macOS*,
https://doi.org/10.1007/978-1-4842-7045-5_10

4. Opening raw sockets

5. Managing processes

6. Reading the contents of virtual memory

7. Changing system settings

8. Loading kernel extensions

9. Storing passwords in the System Keychain

But as discussed earlier, elevated privileges come with an enhanced risk of security vulnerabilities which we will discuss in the next section.

Security Vulnerabilities

The majority of software security vulnerabilities comes into the following set of categories.

Buffer Overflows

A buffer overflow happens when an application attempts to write data past the end or past the beginning of a buffer. It can cause applications to crash, compromise data, and even can provide an attack vector for further privilege escalation to compromise the system as a whole.

Any application that takes input from the user or from a file or from the network needs to store that input, and they store it either in a heap or a stack. Buffer overflow attacks generally compromise either the stack, the heap, or both.

Unvalidated Input

As a best practice, we should check all inputs received by the application to make sure that the data is reasonable. For example, a graphics file can contain an image of resolution 200 by 300 pixels, but it is not reasonable to contain an image that is 200 by –1 pixels. A badly designed application in an attempt to read such a file would try to allocate a buffer of an incorrect size, leading to the potential for a heap overflow attack. Precisely due to these reasons, we must check input data carefully. This process is known as input validation or sanity check.

Any unvalidated input received by the application from an untrusted source is a potential target for attack. In the past, unvalidated inputs have been exploited to steal data, take control of operating systems, corrupt users' disks, and more.

Race Conditions

A race condition happens when changes in the order of occurrence of two or more events can cause a change in behavior. A hacker can take advantage of the situation to insert malicious code to interfere with the normal operation of the application. Hence, the race condition is a security vulnerability. Attackers sometimes take advantage of small time gaps in the processing of code to interfere with the sequence of operations to exploit them.

Insecure File Operations

In addition to time-of-check–time-of-use problems, many other file operations are insecure. An application which makes assumptions about the location, ownership, or other attributes of a file is most vulnerable to these types of attacks. For example, an application might assume that it can always write to a file created by the application itself. However, if a hacker somehow changes the permissions or flags on that file, and if the application does not check the result after a write operation, it will not detect the file tampering.

Access Control Problems

Much of the discussion on security vulnerabilities in the software security is in terms of privileges, and lots of exploits involve a hacker somehow acquiring more privileges than they should have. Privileges are access rights granted by the operating system, thus controlling who is allowed to read and write files, directories, and so on.

Hackers are particularly interested in the gaining of root privileges, which means having the unrestricted permission to perform any operation on the system. An application running with root privileges can access everything and change anything. Many security vulnerabilities are a result of programming errors that allow a hacker to obtain root privileges. Some attacks involve having access to system files that should be restricted or finding a weak point in a program, for example, an application installer, that is already running with root privileges. Due to these reasons, it's important to always run programs with as few privileges as possible. Also, when it is necessary to run a program with elevated privileges, we should do so for as short a time as possible.

There are multiple ways to enforce access controls like authenticating before granting authorization to perform an operation, using digital certificates, and so on.

Principle of Least Privilege in Hostile Environment

If a user has logged in with restricted privileges, then the application should also run with those restricted privileges, thus effectively limiting the amount of damage an attacker can do, even after successfully hacking the application into running malicious code. We should not assume that the user is logged in with administrator privileges and should be prepared with a helper application with elevated privileges if a task demands so.

The idea of limiting risk by limiting access to the system goes back to the "need to know" policy followed by government security agencies. In software security, this policy is often called the principle of least privilege.

The principle of least privilege states

Every program and every user of the system should operate using the least set of privileges necessary to complete the job.

—Saltzer, J.H. and Schroeder, M.D., "The Protection of Information in Computer Systems," Proceedings of the IEEE, vol. 63, no. 9, Sept 1975.

In practical, the principle of least privilege means that we should avoid running as root, but if you absolutely must run as root to perform some task, you should run a separate helper application to perform the privileged task. Also, to the extent possible, the software should run in a sandbox, thus restricting its privileges even further.

By running with the least privilege possible, we can limit damage from accidents or errors, including malicious events.

This also reduces chances of unintentional, unwanted, and improper uses of privilege.

We must know that, even if our code is free of errors, vulnerabilities in any libraries our code links to can be used to attack our application.

There are a number of ways listed as follows through which a hacker can take advantage of vulnerabilities if the application is running as root.

Launching a New Process

Any new process runs with the privileges of the process that launched it; if a hacker can trick the application to launch a malicious code, the malicious code runs with the privileges of our application. Hence, if the application is running with root privileges and is vulnerable to attacks, the attacker can easily gain control of the system.

Command-Line Arguments

As all command-line arguments, including the program name (argv[0]), are under the control of the user, we should not trust argv[0] to point to a program. If we use the command line to reexecute an application or a tool, a malicious user might substitute a different app for argv[0], causing the execution of the attacker's code with your privileges.

Inheriting File Descriptors

Any child process inherits its own copy of the parent process's file descriptors. Hence, if you have a handle on a network socket, file, shared memory, or other resources that's pointed to by a file descriptor and you fork off a child process, you must either close the file descriptor or must make sure that the child process cannot be tampered with. Else, a malicious user can use the subprocess to tamper with the resources referenced by the file descriptors.

For example, if you open a password file and don't close it before forking a process, the new child process has access to the password file.

To set a file descriptor so that it closes automatically when you execute a new process, we should use the fcntl system call to set the close-on-exec flag. We must set this flag individually for each file descriptor.

Abusing Environment Variables

A lot of libraries use environment variables which can be vulnerable to be attacked with buffer overflows or by inserting inappropriate values. If the application links to any such libraries, the application becomes prone to attacks through any such compromised environment variables. Worse, if the application is running as root, the hacker might be able to bring down or gain control of the whole system.

Child processes inherit environment variables, and so if we fork off a child process, the parent process should validate the values of all environment variables before using them in case they were altered by the child process.

Modifying Process Limits

We can limit the consumption of system resources by a process using the setrlimit system call. For example, we can set the size of the largest file the process can create, the maximum amount of physical memory a process may use, the maximum amount of CPU time the process can consume, and so on. These process limits are also inherited by child processes.

If a hacker uses setrlimit to alter these limits, it can cause operations to fail when they should have not failed in a normal scenario. A vulnerability was identified in a version of Linux that made it possible for an attacker to limit the size of the /etc/passwd and /etc/shadow files by decreasing the maximum file size. So, the next time a utility tries to access one of these files, it truncated the file resulting in a loss of data and denial of service.

File Operation Interference

If we are running with elevated privileges in order to read or write files in a user's directory or world-writable directory, we must be aware of time-of-check–time-of-use problems.

Writing a Privileged Helper

In most of the cases, we can perform the task without needing elevated privileges. But still if we are convinced that part of our application needs elevated privileges, this section provides information to handle that. To understand the Authorization Services and the proper way to factor an application, see **Authorization Services Programming Guide** (https://developer.apple.com/library/archive/documentation/Security/Conceptual/authorization_concepts/01introduction/introduction.html#//apple_ref/doc/uid/TP30000995) for more details.

It is very important that we check the user's rights to perform the privileged operation, both before and after launching the privileged helper tool. The helper tool with root privileges and the setuid bit set has sufficient privileges to perform all the task needed to perform. However, if the logged in user doesn't have the rights to perform the task, the application shouldn't launch the helper tool, and even if the helper tool gets launched, it should quit without performing the task. So, the non-privileged application before launching the privileged helper tool should first use Authorization Services to determine whether the user is authorized or not and to authenticate the user if necessary, a process called preauthorizing. Before performing the task that requires elevated privileges, the privileged helper tool should authorize the user again. As soon as the task is complete, the privileged helper tool should terminate.

While writing a privileged helper tool, you need to be very careful while making assumptions. For example, it is dangerous to assume that function calls will always be succeeded and to proceed on that assumption. You must be careful to avoid any of the pitfalls like buffer overflows and race conditions.

If possible, avoid linking to any extra libraries. If you have no choice but to use a library, make sure that the library has no security vulnerabilities and also that it doesn't link to any other libraries. In order to make the helper tool as secure as possible, make it to perform very small and dedicated task and then quit. Keeping the life span of a helper tool short makes it less likely to introduce mistakes.

SMJobBless

SMJobBless is a function in the Service Management framework which submits the executable for the given label as a launchd job. SMJobBless removes the need for a setuid helper invoked through AuthorizationExecuteWithPrivileges() in order to install a launchd plist. Success is returned if the job is already installed.

The following requirements must be met in order to use this function:

For the calling application

1. The calling application and target helper tool must both be signed.

2. The calling application's Info.plist must include an "SMPrivilegedExecutables" dictionary of strings. Each string in the dictionary is a textual representation of the code signing requirement used to determine whether the application owns the privileged helper tool once installed or not for subsequent versions to update the installed version.

Each key in SMPrivilegedExecutables is a reverse DNS label for the helper tool which must be globally unique.

For the Helper tool

1. The helper tool must include an embedded Info.plist containing an "SMAuthorizedClients" array of strings. Each string in the dictionary is a textual representation of the code signing requirement describing a client which is allowed to add and remove the tool.

2. The helper tool must include an embedded launchd plist. The label key is the only required key in this plist. When the launchd plist is extracted and written to disk, the key for ProgramArguments will be set to an array of one element pointing to a standard location. We cannot specify our own program arguments, so we should not rely on custom command-line arguments being passed to the tool. Pass parameters if any through IPC.

3. The helper tool must reside in the Contents/Library/ LaunchServices directory inside the application bundle, and its name must be its launchd job label. So if the launchd job label is "com.HemDutt. CustomApp.helper", this must be the name of the helper tool in the application bundle.

Swift Implementation

Enough of theory. It's time to get our hands dirty with code ☺. In the sample code, we will go through with the basics of creating a privileged Helper tool, creating a communication from the client app to the Helper tool using XPC. I will leave the operation to be done through a privileged Helper tool to your imagination. You can try installing some application, copying files in root directories, or saving items in the System Keychain and so on.

OK... Let's get going! I am excited for this.

Note   In order to see the code in this sample working, replace ""**Apple Development: hemdutt@abcXYZ.com (G98C87WTS8)**" **and certificate 1[field.1.2.842.113636.100.6.2.1]**" with the certificate that you use to sign targets.

There are three places where you need to specify the certificate:

1. Client app's Info.plist

2. Privileged Helper's Info.plist

3. Server.swift entitlements constant

The name of the certificate can be found in your login keychain. Double-click the certificate in the list and copy its common name.

Preparing Client and Helper Targets

First, create a macOS App project (Figure 10-1) named "SMJobBlessPrivilegeElevation". We will use the Swift programming language for this sample.

Figure 10-1. macOS App template

By default, it will create a GUI app target with the same name. I changed the target name to "SMJobBlessClient". This target will act as our client application.

As privileged operations are not available for sandboxed applications, we will remove the sandboxed environment from the capabilities section by clicking the "X" button for App Sandbox (Figure 10-2).

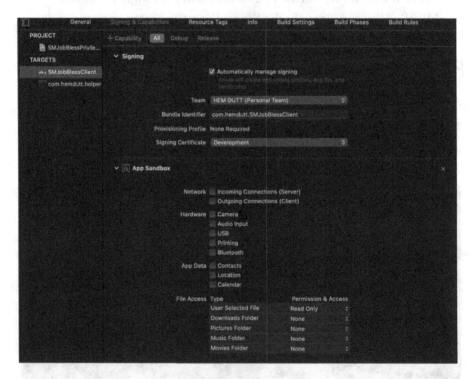

Figure 10-2. *Remove App Sandbox*

Now, we will create a new target (Command Line Tool) for the privileged Helper (Figure 10-3). The product name for this target should be the same as the desired launchd job label which is a unique string that describes the service and is provided by the Helper tool. In order to start the Helper tool, we need to register its label with launchd. A convention is to use the reverse DNS notation, and so I have used the name "com.hemdutt.helper".

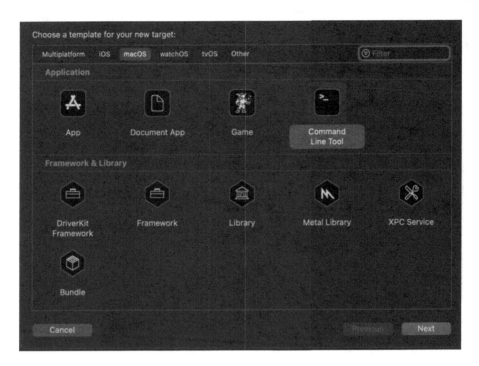

Figure 10-3. *Helper target*

Now let's get back to the client's target and go to "Build Phases." Add
the Helper tool as a dependency as shown in Figure 10-4.

Figure 10-4. *Add the Helper tool as a dependency in the client's
target*

Also, add a new copy file phase and select "Wrapper" Subpath, paste Contents/Library/LaunchServices, and add the Helper application to this Copy Files phase as shown in Figure 10-5.

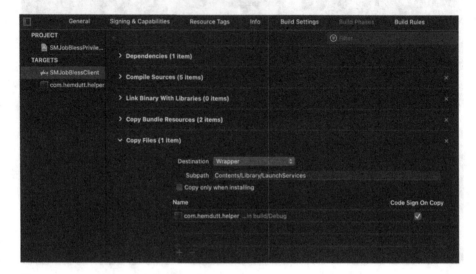

Figure 10-5. *Add the client's build phases*

Setting Up Signing Requirements

Again, let's go back to the Helper's target and add "launchd.plist" (Figure 10-6). In the plist file, add a Label key with a launchd job label value and add a MachServices key with a Dictionary type. Add there a key-value pair with a launchd job label as a key and YES Boolean as a value as shown in Figure 10-6.

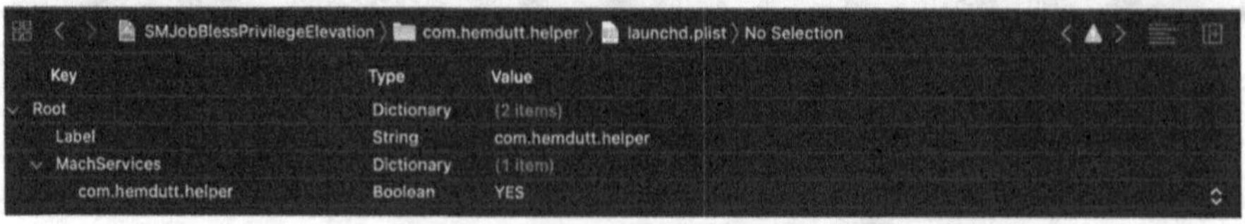

Figure 10-6. *launchd.plist*

Now add "Info.plist" (Figure 10-7) in the Helper's target and

1. Add CFBundleIdentifier and paste $(PRODUCT_
    BUNDLE_IDENTIFIER) as its bundle identifier.

2. Add CFBundleInfoDictionaryVersion with string
    value 6.0.

3. Add an SMAuthorizedClients key with an array of
    strings type to Info.plist. Every entry in this array
    is a description for signing requirements for each
    client, for example, "identifier "com.hemdutt.
    SMJobBlessClient" and anchor apple generic and
    certificate leaf[subject.CN] = "Apple Development:
    hemdutt@abcXYZ.com (G98C87WTS8)" and
    certificate 1[field.1.2.842.113636.100.6.2.1]".

Figure 10-7. *Helper's Info.plist*

Open the Helper's Build Settings and find the setting "Info.plist File".
Set the path to the Helper's Info.plist **$(SRCROOT)/$(TARGET_NAME)/
Info.plist**.

We need to build Info.plist into the resulting binary file. For that, we
need to set another Build Setting, that is, "Create Info.plist Section in
Binary", to YES as shown in Figure 10-8.

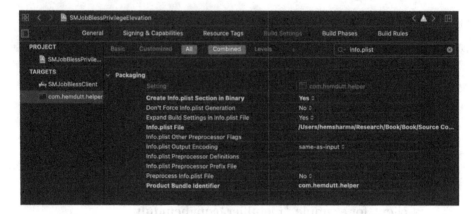

Figure 10-8. *Helper's build settings for Info.plist*

To embed the launchd.plist file into the Helper binary file, go to Build Settings and find "Other Linker Flags" as shown in Figure 10-9.

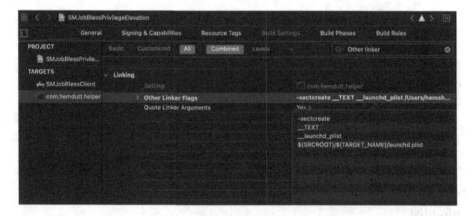

Figure 10-9. *Helper's build settings for launchd.plist*

Add statements for the Linker Flags in order as shown in Listing 10-1.

Listing 10-1. Helper's build setting for launchd.plist

```
-sectcreate
__TEXT
__launchd_plist
$(SRCROOT)/${TARGET_NAME}/launchd.plist
```

Now coming back to the client target, as shown in Figure 10-10, add an SMPrivilegedExecutables key with type Dictionary in the client's Info.plist and then add there a key-value pair with

Key = launchd job label (in our case "com.hemdutt.helper")

Value = signing requirements (in our case "identifier "com.hemdutt. helper" and anchor apple generic and certificate leaf[subject.CN] = "Apple Development: hemdutt@abcXYZ.com (G98C87WTS8)" and certificate 1[field.1.2.842.113636.100.6.2.1]")

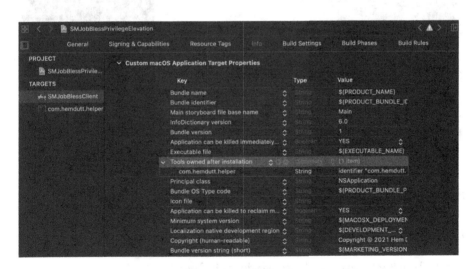

Figure 10-10. *Client's signing requirements*

With this, we are done with the signing requirements. Now let's focus on the code.

Shared Code

There will be some code which will be shared between the client and the
Helper. We will put this type of code in the "Shared" group (Figure 10-11).
All files in this group will have a target membership of both client and
helper apps as shown in Figure 10-11. First, create a swift file "Constants.
swift" and create a constant for the launchd job label as shown in
Listing 10-2.

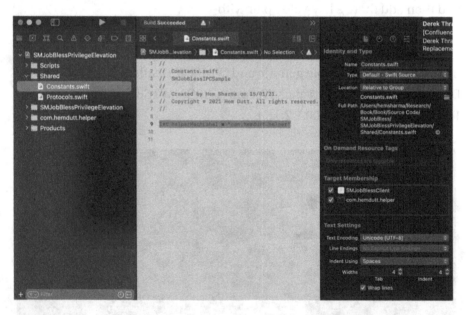

Figure 10-11. *Shared Code*

Listing 10-2. Shared constants

```
let helperMachLabel = "com.hemdutt.helper"
```

The next category of shared code is the protocols used by the client
and the Helper to communicate with each other. For this, create another
swift file "Protocols.swift" and add two protocols in that as shown in
Listings 10-3 and 10-4.

Listing 10-3. Include in Protocols.swift

```
import Foundation
```

Listing 10-4. Protocols in Protocols.swift

```
@objc protocol PrivilegedProtocol
{
    func privilegedOperation()
}

@objc public protocol PrivilegedClient
{
    func privilegedOperationFinished(description: String?)
}
```

Client Implementation

Now, as we are done with the shared code, let's look into the code at the client side. To create an XPC connection with the Helper, we will first create a class "Client." For this, we will create a swift file "Client.swift" in client code. Include Foundation framework as shown in Listing 10-5.

Listing 10-5. Include in Client.swift

```
import Foundation
```

In the Client class, we will write code to create an XPC connection with the Helper and also to capture any connection interruption if it happened as shown in Listing 10-6.

Listing 10-6. Client class in Client.swift

```
class Client
{
    //XPC connection
    var connection: NSXPCConnection?

    func start()
    {
        connection = NSXPCConnection(machServiceName:
        helperMachLabel,
                                        options: .privileged)

        connection?.exportedInterface = NSXPCInterface(with:
        PrivilegedClient.self)
        connection?.exportedObject =
        PrivilegedClientImplementor()
        connection?.remoteObjectInterface =
        NSXPCInterface(with: PrivilegedProtocol.self)

        connection?.invalidationHandler =
        connectionInvalidationHandler
        connection?.interruptionHandler =
        connetionInterruptionHandler

        connection?.resume()

        let service = connection?.remoteObjectProxy as?
        PrivilegedProtocol

        service?.privilegedOperation()
    }
```

```
private func connetionInterruptionHandler()
{
    print("\(type(of: self)): XPC connection has been
    interrupted")
}

private func connectionInvalidationHandler()
{
    print("\(type(of: self)): XPC connection has been
    invalidated XPC")
}
}
```

For capturing the event when the Helper finishes, we will create an extension of the Client class, as shown in Listing 10-7, inheriting the "PrivilegedClient" protocol described in Listing 10-4.

Listing 10-7. Client extension in Client.swift

```
class PrivilegedClientImplementor: NSObject, PrivilegedClient
{
    func privilegedOperationFinished(description: String?)
    {
        print("Finished privileged operation: \(#function)")
    }
}
```

Now look at the consumer code at the client side. In a view controller, we will use the "Client" class to start the Helper for executing the privileged operation as shown in Listings 10-8 and 10-9.

Listing 10-8. Imports in the view controller

```
import Cocoa
import SecurityFoundation
import ServiceManagement
```

Listing 10-9. Bless Helper

```
class ViewController: NSViewController
{
    var client = Client()

    override func viewDidLoad()
    {
        super.viewDidLoad()

        guard let auth = self.authorize() else
        {
            fatalError("Authorization not acquired.")
        }

        _ = self.blessHelper(label: helperMachLabel,
        authorization: auth)
        client.start()
    }

    private func authorize() -> AuthorizationRef?
    {

        var auth: AuthorizationRef?
        let status: OSStatus = AuthorizationCreate(nil, nil,
        [], &auth)
```

```
    if status != errAuthorizationSuccess
    {
        NSLog("Client App: Authorization failed with status
        code \(status)")

        return nil
    }

    return auth
}

private func blessHelper(label: String, authorization:
AuthorizationRef) -> Bool
{

    var error: Unmanaged<CFError>?
    let blessStatus = SMJobBless(kSMDomainSystemLaunchd,
    label as CFString, authorization, &error)

    if !blessStatus
    {
        NSLog("Client App: Helper bless failed with error
        \(error!.takeUnretainedValue())")
    }

    return blessStatus
    }
}
```

With this, we are done with the client infrastructure to invoke a
helper for performing privileged tasks. Next, let's look at the Helper tool's
implementation.

Privileged Helper Tool Implementation

To start with the Helper tool implementation, we will create a Server class which will be responsible for validating the client and communicating with the client as shown in Listing 10-11. But first import Foundation framework as shown in Listing 10-10.

Listing 10-10. Import in Server.swift

```
import Foundation
```

Listing 10-11. Server class in Server.swift

```
class Server: NSObject
{
    internal static let sharedInstance = Server()

    private var listener: NSXPCListener?
    // Here I have copied the requirements from the Info.plist
        for removing complexity
    // in a commercial application you can want to put
        the requirements in one place like in preprocessor
        definitions
    private let entitlements = "identifier \"com.hemdutt.
    SMJobBlessClient\" and anchor apple generic and
    certificate leaf[subject.CN] = \"Apple Development:
    hemdutt@abcXYZ.com (G98C87WTS8)\" and certificate 1[
    field.1.2.842.113636.100.6.2.1]"

    internal func start()
    {
        listener = NSXPCListener(machServiceName:
        helperMachLabel)
        listener?.delegate = self
```

```
    listener?.resume()
}

private func connetionInterruptionHandler()
{
    print("Helper: Connection Interrupted")
}

private func connectionInvalidationHandler()
{
    print("Helper: Connection Invalidated")
}

private func isValidClient(forConnection connection:
NSXPCConnection) -> Bool
{

    var token = connection.auditToken;
    let tokenData = Data(bytes: &token, count:
    MemoryLayout.size(ofValue:token))
    let attributes = [kSecGuestAttributeAudit : tokenData]

    let flags: SecCSFlags = []
    var code: SecCode? = nil
    var status = SecCodeCopyGuestWithAttributes(nil,
    attributes as CFDictionary, flags, &code)

    guard status == errSecSuccess, let dynamicCode = code
    else
    {
        return false
    }
```

```
    var requirement: SecRequirement?

    status = SecRequirementCreateWithString(entitlements as
    CFString, flags, &requirement)

    guard status == errSecSuccess else
    {
        return false
    }

    status = SecCodeCheckValidity(dynamicCode, flags,
    requirement)
    return status == errSecSuccess
  }
}
```

Implement NSXPCListenerDelegate to listen to the connection. For
that, we will write an extension of the Server class as shown in Listing 10-12.

Listing 10-12. Server extension in Server.swift

```
extension Server: NSXPCListenerDelegate
{

    func listener(_ listener: NSXPCListener,
    shouldAcceptNewConnection newConnection: NSXPCConnection)
    -> Bool
    {

        if (!isValidClient(forConnection: newConnection))
        {
            NSLog("Helper: Client is not valid")
            return false
        }
```

```
print("Helper: Client is valid")

let service = PrivilegedService()

newConnection.exportedInterface = NSXPCInterface(with:
PrivilegedProtocol.self)
newConnection.exportedObject = service

newConnection.remoteObjectInterface =
NSXPCInterface(with: PrivilegedClient.self)

newConnection.interruptionHandler =
connetionInterruptionHandler
newConnection.invalidationHandler =
connectionInvalidationHandler

newConnection.resume()

service.client = newConnection.remoteObjectProxy as?
PrivilegedClient

        return true
    }
}
```

After completing our Server implementation, we will create another file "PrivilegedService.swift" to actually perform privileged tasks and inform the client on the completion of tasks. This class will inherit the "PrivilegedProtocol" described in Listing 10-4.

Let's look at the implementation of the PrivilegedService class in Listings 10-13 and 10-14.

Listing 10-13. Import in PrivilegedService.swift

```
import Foundation
```

Listing 10-14. PrivilegedService class in Server.swift

```swift
class PrivilegedService: NSObject, PrivilegedProtocol
{
    var client: PrivilegedClient?

    func privilegedOperation()
    {
        //Perform privileged tasks here
        print("Helper: \(#function)")
        client?.privilegedOperationFinished(description:
        "Finished privilege operation")
    }
}
```

Now, create an extension of the NSXPCConnection class and declare a variable of type "audit_token_t". This is used by Apple to internally verify the XPC connection as shown in Listing 10-15.

Listing 10-15. Extension for NSXPCConnection

```objc
#import <Foundation/Foundation.h>

@interface NSXPCConnection (AuditToken)

@property (nonatomic, readonly) audit_token_t auditToken;

@end
```

This extension will be an Objective-C header file; we will also make an entry in the helper's bridging header for the file as well.

Now to finish our Helper tool implementation, go to main.swift and start the server as shown in Listing 10-16.

Listing 10-16. main.swift

```swift
import Foundation

NSLog("Privileged Helper has started")

Server.sharedInstance.start()

CFRunLoopRun()
```

With this, we are done with the Helper tool implementation and good to go with our privileged task execution.

Running Privileged Operation

To test run the final code and our implementation for the privileged helper tool, run the code for the client app target. The client app on launch will try to install the privileged helper tool and will prompt the user for permissions (Figure 10-12).

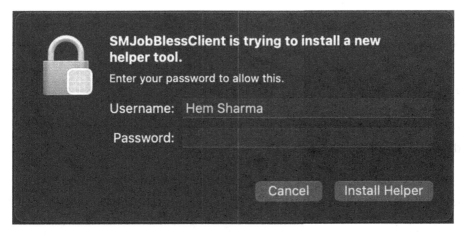

Figure 10-12. *Installing priviledged helper*

Enter the password and let the client app install the Helper tool. Next, the client app, after installing the Helper tool successfully, will call the privileged operation in the Helper tool. From there, after finishing the privileged operation, the Helper tool will call **func privilegedOperationFinished** in **class PrivilegedClientImplementor** written inside the **Client.swift** file.

We can analyze console logs to check if the communication between the client app and the Helper tool succeeded or not.

Error Logs

If the signing setup described in section "Setting Up Signing Requirements" is not followed correctly, the communication between the client app and the Helper tool will fail with error as shown in Listing 10-17. On the other hand, if the setup is correct, you will see a success log as shown in Listing 10-18.

Listing 10-17. Error logs

```
SMJobBlessClient[28730:4739447] Client App: Helper bless failed
with error Error Domain=CFErrorDomainLaunchd Code=4 "(null)"
```

Listing 10-18. Success logs

```
Finished privileged operation: privilegedOperationFinished(
description:)
```

In case you are struggling with signing setup errors, the Python script mentioned in the next section will come in handy to resolve this issue.

Python Script

As you must have observed, there are lots of nuances to remember for preparing the overall structure for a privileged helper tool. In order to help the developers, Apple provides a Python script SMJobBlessUtil.py, which I have included in the Scripts group in the sample project. It offers two functions:

check: It allows to find mistakes in the setup. Just run path/to/ SMJobBlessUtil.py check path/to/built/application.

An example is shown in Listing 10-19.

Listing 10-19. check

```
hemsharma ~ % /Users/hemsharma/Research/Book/Book/Source\ Code/
SMJobBless/SMJobBlessPrivilegeElevation/Scripts/SMJobBlessUtil.
py check /Users/hemsharma/Library/Developer/Xcode/DerivedData/
SMJobBlessPrivilegeElevation-hccdvotvviftpbaaomgqwmhtmrfz/
Build/Products/Debug/SMJobBlessClient.app
```

setreq: It allows to update Info.plist files in order to fulfill the requirements. Run it like this: setreq /path/to/app /path/to/app/Info.plist /path/to/tool/Info.plist.

An example is shown in Listing 10-20.

Listing 10-20. setreq

```
hemsharma ~ % /Users/hemsharma/Research/Book/Book/Source\ Code/
SMJobBless/SMJobBlessPrivilegeElevation/Scripts/SMJobBlessUtil.
py setreq /Users/hemsharma/Library/Developer/Xcode/DerivedData/
SMJobBlessPrivilegeElevation-hccdvotvviftpbaaomgqwmhtmrfz/
Build/Products/Debug/SMJobBlessClient.app /Users/
hemsharma/Research/Book/Book/Source\ Code/SMJobBless/
SMJobBlessPrivilegeElevation/SMJobBlessPrivilegeElevation/
```

```
Info.plist /Users/hemsharma/Research/Book/Book/Source\ Code/
SMJobBless/SMJobBlessPrivilegeElevation/com.hemdutt.helper/
Info.plist
```

These scripts prove to be really handy while fixing the code signing requirement issues.

Real-World Scenarios for Creating Secure Privileged Helper Tool

As discussed before in this chapter, by default applications on macOS run with the privileges of the currently logged in user. Majority of tasks on macOS can be executed with admin privileges, but there are a few operations that require additional privileges above and beyond the scope of even an admin user. For example, if you are creating a VPN client and want to store VPN credentials in the System Keychain, you need to run the application as root, which is inherently insecure. So, the better approach would be to create a privileged helper to carry out this operation only. Another good example is installing another application through your application which again needs root privileges. In this case, it is advisable to use the privileged helper tool to carry out the operation. Any other scenarios which involve enhanced privileges should use the helper tool.

What's Next?

With this, we come to the *end* of our journey on interprocess communication on macOS. Hope you enjoyed and learned as much as I enjoyed while writing. Let me know through feedbacks what next topic we can discuss. Till then, happy learning!

Conclusion

This book is intended for Software Engineers designing and developing secure and modular applications on macOS. This book explores all the **Inter-process communication (IPC)** techniques and **Privilege separation/elevation** techniques available on macOS.

Whether you are maintaining legacy code in Objective-C or writing a new code in Swift, this book has sample codes in both languages to help you in implementing IPC and Privilege elevation securely.

Building a highly modular software is always tricky and complexity only increases when the program is interacting with another program. If the **Inter-process communication (IPC)** is poorly conceived and carried out, it can lead to severe security risks not just for the participating programs but for the overall system. A poorly conceived IPC can expose the entire system for the hackers and other over the network attacks.

Inter-process communication (IPC) is defined as set of techniques used for exchanging data or message among multiple threads in one or more processes. Processes may be running on one or more computers connected by a network or running locally.

On **macOS,** there are multiple scenarios where implementing IPC between two or more processes/applications is necessary. These scenarios can be broadly categorised into five categories i.e. Information sharing, Computational Speedup, Modularity, Convenience and Privilege Separation.

We'll explore all techniques available for IPC from the kernel level to the high level macOS layers, while applying theoretical concepts into practical implementations on real world scenarios.

© Hem Dutt 2021
H. Dutt, *Interprocess Communication with macOS*,
https://doi.org/10.1007/978-1-4842-7045-5

After completing this book you will be able to

- Expand capabilities of your program by sharing data within multiple applications.

- Understand and dig deep into the world of Helper tools to create apps which need privilege elevation like a VPN client etc.

- Enhance modularity of your system by allowing your application to interact and share data with your website.

- Implement theoretical concepts of IPC to solve real world problems.

Index

© Hem Dutt 2021
H. Dutt, *Interprocess Communication with macOS*,
https://doi.org/10.1007/978-1-4842-7045-5

Printed in the United States
by Baker & Taylor Publisher Services